The Entrepreneur's Journey

How to make your business work for you

David Coffaro

The Entrepreneur's Journey

The Entrepreneur's Journey
How to Make your Business Work for You

© 2026 David Coffaro
All Rights Reserved
Published by SACG United States

ISBN: 978-1-7344099-3-2

All rights reserved. No part of this publication may be reproduced, stored in a retrieval system, or transmitted in any form by any means, electronic, mechanical, photocopy, recording, or any other (except for brief quotations in printed reviews), without the written permission of the publisher.

captures his deep understanding of how entrepreneurs can build partnerships and leverage resources across public, private, and education sectors to unlock opportunity and scale growth. This book is an invaluable guide for anyone dedicated to building a thriving, sustainable business.

John P. Keisler, CEO & Managing Partner, Sunstone Investment Group

Entrepreneurship demands more than a good idea. It requires discipline, clarity, and the ability to lead through continuous change. In The Entrepreneur's Journey, Dave Coffaro distills those fundamentals into a practical and accessible framework that founders can apply at any stage. I would recommend this book to entrepreneurs committed to building businesses that are both resilient and intentional.

Carol Ornstein, Founder & CEO, Clear Path Methodology

Dave's new book, The Entrepreneur's Journey, is a must-read for entrepreneurs and small business owners looking to reach the next level of success. It serves as a practical guide going back to the basics of business — what I like to call the "Big Fundamentals."

As an entrepreneur myself, I found this book deeply relatable. Dave's insight that we need to "focus on the small fundamental things in order for the big things to matter" was a refreshing reminder of what truly drives business growth. This is exactly the kind of book I needed - one that helps me understand how to run my business better, instead of letting my business run me.

Jay Ungos, President and Founder, "X" Business Network-XBN

At Tech Coast Venture Network, we see many founders fail to secure funding because they haven't earned relevance or clearly articulated why they matter to the market. David Coffaro's The Entrepreneur's Journey offers the solution to this problem, providing the strategic process that builds investor confidence. It is a must-read for any entrepreneur ready to scale by letting a proven processes replace founder-mode heroics.

Tony Crisp President of Tech Coast Venture Network and CEO of CRISPx Brand Marketing Agency

The Entrepreneur's Journey is a thoughtful guide for leaders who want to build businesses that are both relevant today and resilient for the future. Dave Coffaro blends customer insight, competitive strategy, and practical decision-making into clear frameworks that help entrepreneurs move from reacting to intentionally designing what comes next. His emphasis on understanding who your customer is, why they would pay, and why they would pay now is both simple and profound, which is incredibly useful in today's fast-changing environment. As both a legacy business owner and entrepreneur, I found myself nodding along and already applying his ideas in my own work. Dave's work is especially valuable for founders and next-generation leaders navigating growth and change.

Jenny Dinnen, MacKenzie & Next Gen Collaborative

In a world obsessed with headlines and hype, *The Entrepreneur's Journey* brings us back to what truly drives durable success: fundamentals. Dave Coffaro reminds entrepreneurs that disciplined execution, customer clarity, and daily intentional action are what bring results. This is a practical, grounded handbook for founders who want to build businesses that actually work for them.

Juliana Elstad, Multi-time MedTech CEO, Board Director, and Entrepreneur

The key to success is planning and building a solid strategic foundation for your business. In *The Entrepreneur's Journey*, Dave Coffaro provides insightful advice and real-world examples you need to drive growth. Read it for actionable tactics on customer engagement, go-to-market, change management, and executive leadership that will ensure your execution leads to success.

Scott Fox, CEO of StartupCouncil.org

The Entrepreneur's Journey is a grounded, no-nonsense guide to what it really takes to build and scale a business. Dave Coffaro brings clarity to the fundamentals of customer focus, disciplined execution, and constant refinement, that many entrepreneurs overlook. This is a practical playbook for leaders who want to create relevance, not just growth. Dave offers practical insights and real-world perspectives that help founders build businesses with purpose, resilience, and staying power. It's a smart, actionable read for entrepreneurs at any stage.

Rebecca Hall, President and CEO, Idea Hall

With thousands of leadership books coming out every year, and "experts" on every corner lining up to help you start your business, it is refreshing to have a book like "*The Entrepreneur's Journey*" by my friend Dave Coffaro as a resource for all of us who have had "that idea" for a business, but did not know where to start. Dave has given us a master class in how to take our idea, turn into action, and then move it a business that can sustain, grow, and have a real impact. He has done this, he has led others in doing this, and now he is taking his experience and success and is sharing it with anyone who wants to move from thinking, to doing, to impact. Anyone serious about starting up or growing their business should read this book, and implement the strategies, stories, and tools you will find.

Ed Hart, Founder & President, The Hart Leadership Group

David Coffaro has long been a trusted leader in empowering small businesses and entrepreneurs across Southern California. *The Entrepreneur's Journey*

Introduction

Table of Contents

Introduction An actionable handbook for early stage, scaling, and stuck entrepreneurs ix

Chapter 1 From Idea to Entrepreneurship..................................1

Chapter 2 Know your Customer and How to Serve Them.............9

Chapter 3 Plan, Adjust, Repeat 19

Chapter 4 Go to Market Model Management 37

Chapter 5 Effective Entrepreneurial Leadership 65

Chapter 6 Working ON Your Business 75

Chapter 7 Why You? 105

Chapter 8 The Entrepreneur as Change Leader 113

Chapter 9 Closing thoughts: The Entrepreneur's Operating System 137

The Entrepreneur's Journey

Introduction

Introduction
An actionable handbook for early stage, scaling, and stuck entrepreneurs

The *Macaroni Journal* article highlighted construction of a new, state-of-the-art factory in Rockford, Illinois. The new pasta manufacturing site enabled its operators to more than double their previous production level by manufacturing on the ground floor level, then drying noodles on upper floors of the three-story building.

The article noted the business owner's ambition to move from a small facility into a significantly larger one capable of producing dozens of barrels of fresh pasta products daily. This expansion was welcome news after a handful of less-than-successful entrepreneurial endeavors by these founders.

To the casual *Macaroni Journal* reader, it was simply business news. To my grandparents, it marked the visible beginning of a mindset that would carry across generations of our family.

Entrepreneurship rarely starts with a grand announcement. More often, it begins quietly, with an idea, taking a risk, and demonstrating willingness to build something where nothing existed before. For my family, that moment came nearly a century ago in Rockford, Illinois, when my grandfather, Vincent Coffaro, and his partner, my great uncle Carl Durante, ventured to build a new pasta manufacturing business from the ground up.

The Entrepreneur's Journey

They were not celebrities, venture-funded founders, or Silicon Valley disruptors. They were practical entrepreneurs - immigrants building stability through hard work, calculated risk, strong faith, and belief in their vision.

That example became more than family history; it became a blueprint. Subsequent generations, me included, absorbed an unspoken lesson: entrepreneurship is not just about starting companies. It's about initiative, resilience, adaptation, and the courage to act before conditions feel perfect. The industries have changed, the tools are different, but the underlying principles remain remarkably consistent.

For me, the entrepreneurial journey included starting and operating my own businesses, as well as operating as an entrepreneur in the corporate arena. The same blueprint continues with my children as they demonstrate the entrepreneurial spirit in their chosen fields.

The Entrepreneur's Journey: How to Make your Business Work for You discusses some of the most common challenges to entrepreneurship and how to navigate them, from translating an idea into an enterprise (solopreneur or multiple employees), developing an effective go-to-market model, growth, ongoing refinement, and investing time working on (not just in your business) your business.

Why entrepreneurship? An entrepreneur is one who starts or invests in a business, typically assuming the risks and potential rewards. Entrepreneurs are often innovators, introducing new ideas, products, services, or ways of doing business that drive progress and change.

Entrepreneurship has been a driving force behind economic and social progress for centuries, evolving from small-scale trade

Introduction

in ancient civilizations to today's high-impact global ventures. In early societies, entrepreneurs were merchants, artisans, and farmers who uncovered opportunities to create value through commerce and innovation. Two centuries ago, the Industrial Revolution triggered a pivotal shift as entrepreneurship became closely linked with manufacturing, technological advancements, and the birth of new, scalable business practices.

Over time, entrepreneurship has become more accessible due to broadly available technologies and evolution of cultural attitudes toward innovation and risk-taking. Social media platforms and Covid-era acceptance of remote work led to a new phase of innovation and entrepreneurship, seeding job creation, driving economic growth, and empowering individuals to bring new business ideas to life.

Entrepreneurship doesn't begin with a pitch deck, valuation, or bold vision statement. These ingredients matter, but there is foundational work that must take place first. The Entrepreneur's Journey begins with fundamentals, which inform small, repeatable actions, performed with intention and discipline. Mastery is not built in moments of inspiration or innovation; it is built through constant improvement in the basics.

There's an often-told story about legendary UCLA basketball coach, John Wooden, who opened each season by teaching his players how to put on their socks and properly lace and tie their shoes. Not because they didn't already know how, but because excellence demands revisiting fundamentals. Details matter. Small missteps compound. And no one, no matter how innovative or talented, is above the basics.

Entrepreneurship works the same way. Founders often bypass essentials in pursuit of delivering their minimum viable product, obtaining funding, or recognition. They market their offering before developing customer clarity, seek growth before operational discipline, and acclaim before execution. But the truth is simple: if you don't do the small, fundamental things well, the big things won't matter.

This book is about the fundamentals. *The Entrepreneur's Journey: How to Make your Business Work for You* is an actionable handbook for early stage, scaling, and stuck entrepreneurs. It is about mastering your craft through constant improvement, always remembering who you work for. It is about refining fundamentals until they become instinct, not because they are glamorous, but because they are essential.

Entrepreneurial success is not an event, it is a byproduct of preparation, discipline, and fundamentals practiced daily, quietly, and relentlessly. The pages that follow do not provide a shortcut. They offer something better - a foundation to make your business work for you.

The fundamentals:
- Know your customer
- Plan, adjust, repeat
- Deliver a clear go-to-market model, adjusted as conditions change
- Effective entrepreneurial leadership
- Work consistently ON your business
- Clear value proposition
- Own change leadership

My purpose in writing this book is to provide actionable ideas that help entrepreneurs build from these fundamentals. Context for the entrepreneur's journey fundamentals are a clear destination (success definition, or "vision") and initial route

Introduction

(strategy). Fundamentals remain constant. Your business's success definition may evolve, though slowly, if at all. Strategy will change because business operating conditions on the entrepreneur's journey are in perpetual motion, requiring continuous refinement to the route. Absent understanding that business operating conditions are in perpetual motion, entrepreneurs can be lulled into perceiving change management as an event instead of an ongoing process. Change leadership is an essential capability for entrepreneurs enabling the navigator to observe continually evolving conditions, adapt their route in alignment with their destination, and continue adjustment throughout their journey.

My work – as an entrepreneur, executive, consultant, executive coach, and board member - focuses on guiding people and organizations in navigating the continually evolving business operating environment. This means I am a student of how best to practice agility in a perpetually changing world. I am blessed to be surrounded by wonderful people who inspire me, teach me, and challenge me to be my best self, personally and professionally, with family at the top of this list. Carrie, Michael, Nicole, thank you for sharing ideas, your support, and candid feedback. To my parents and grandparents, I am grateful for the entrepreneurial passion you passed along to me.

My deep gratitude to the entrepreneurs and friends who generously invested time to review *The Entrepreneur's Journey*: Tony Crisp, President of Tech Coast Venture Network and CEO of CRISPx Brand Marketing Agency, Jenny Dinnen, MacKenzie & Next Gen Collaborative, Juliana Elstad, Multi-time MedTech CEO, Board Director, and Entrepreneur, Scott Fox, CEO of StartupCouncil.org, Rebecca Hall, President and CEO, Idea

The Entrepreneur's Journey

Hall, Ed Hart, Founder & President, The Hart Leadership Group, John P. Keisler, CEO & Managing Partner, Sunstone Investment Group, Carol Ornstein, Founder & CEO, Clear Path Methodology, and Jay Ungos, President and Founder, "X" Business Network-XBN. Lee Pound, thank you for your guidance and attention to detail. Rob Kirby, you are an amazing, gifted artist and I'm grateful for your work and our friendship.

To my colleagues and clients – I am blessed by the abundance of lessons and opportunities you share. I am grateful for my opportunity to serve with the Greater Irvine Chamber of Commerce, which has deepened my belief that entrepreneurship is the foundation of a thriving economy, individual fulfillment, and prosperity. My hope: *The Entrepreneur's Journey: How to Make your Business Work for You* becomes a valuable resource for you in your entrepreneur's journey!

Chapter 1
From Idea to Entrepreneurship

Every successful business starts with an idea, but not every idea leads to a successful business. One of the most common myths in entrepreneurship is that a great idea is all it takes. In reality, the journey from idea to functioning enterprise involves clarity, action, continuous refinement, and strong execution of the fundamentals described in the Introduction. It requires deep understanding, not just about your offering (product, service), but of your customer, your own capabilities and competencies, and the broader context in which your business will operate.

This chapter explores the first step of the Innovator's Journey - how to take your idea and translate it into a viable business model. Two core truths to consider:

- As an entrepreneur, you don't work for yourself, you work for your customer.
- For every stage in the growth of your business (and in your career), you must know and build upon your own strengths to optimize your contribution.

The Idea – What Problem Do You Solve?

An idea, on its own, is not a business. A business solves a problem in a way that can be monetized. In Chapter 2, we will cover the importance of knowing your customer. For now, the point for consideration is this: To create a sustainable business, the entrepreneur must clearly understand the problem to be solved or the need to be addressed, in a manner for which customers will perceive value and pay for the offering. Absent a customer perceiving value for which they will pay, the offering is a hobby, not a business.

All Ideas Are Not Equal

Consider this. Two innovators come up with the same product idea - a mobile app that helps users plan and prepare meals based on what's already in their refrigerator. One app launches, and no one seems to care. The other builds a loyal following and scales to thousands of paying users.

What made the difference? It wasn't the idea itself. It was how that idea aligned with a specific customer need, how the prototype was tested with target market users, refined, promoted, and delivered.

Validate Before You Build

In Doug Evans' words, his company, Juicero, "was on a mission to invent products, services and experiences to help people consume the fresh foods that manifest true health and longevity." Evans saw his parents and brother experience significant health issues which shortened their lives and decided to take up a healthier lifestyle. He adopted a raw vegan diet and embraced the benefits of cold-pressed juices.

Evans' enthusiasm inspired him to invest in Organic Avenue, the first cold-pressed juice store in New York. After a decade, Organic Avenue was sold in 2012. Even though the business had sold, Evans missed his cold-pressed juices. His personal desire for healthy juices led him to develop a new concept – Juicero. After a dozen prototypes over three years, Doug Evans developed a state-of-the-art, high tech juicing machine, with a retail price of $700.

From Idea to Entrepreneurship

He launched Juicero on March 31, 2016. The offering included small bags loaded with freshly chopped fruits and vegetables which users placed in the juicing machine, then high force pressed. Fresh food fruit and vegetable bags cost between $5 and $8 each and had a shelf life of about a week.

The Juicero was internet and WiFi enabled with a QR code reader to capture information on each fresh fruit and vegetable bag. This informed users about where the fruits and vegetables came from, as well as health benefits of the cold pressed juice they were about to enjoy.

By the time Juicero went to market, Evans had created a tremendous buzz about the product. The company raised more than $100 million in venture capital from top-tier investors. He wrote a compelling pitch: - restaurant-quality, cold-pressed juice at home, with perfectly measured ingredients and no mess.

Unfortunately, Juicero attempted to solve a problem potential customers didn't have. Consumers didn't see the value in spending $700 for a machine that was big, bulky, and could only use proprietary fruit and vegetable refill packs. Further diminishing the Juicero value proposition, in April, 2017, Bloomberg business reports, Ellen Huet and Olivia Zaleski released their investigation into the product. Their analysis suggested the product was expensive and unnecessary. They found the fruit and vegetable packs could be squeezed by hand and produce almost the same amount of juice as fast as the machine.

In late 2017, Juicero ceased operations. The company's founder had an idea he was passionate about. He developed an interesting product that had no market. Potential customers didn't see the benefit of the product and were not willing to pay a premium price for the Juicero.

It's common for founders to fall in love with their ideas before answering the critical question: *Is this solving a problem or addressing a need people care about?* Before writing code, buying inventory, building a new product, raising capital, or leasing office space, test your business assumptions.

- **What is the problem we are solving, or need we're addressing?** Are people actively seeking a solution to address this need? Are people willing to pay for resolution of this need? Are other firms seeing and addressing this need, and if so, how will I differentiate my offering?
- **Is addressing this need urgent or important?** If the problem or need is considered significant by the target audience, demand will likely be strong; conversely, low urgency needs generally correspond to low demand.
- **Will someone pay to solve it?** Interest is not the same as intent to purchase, and innovation does not automatically create demand. Customers pay to solve real problems or satisfy true needs, not to admire engineering.

Translating Ideas to Entrepreneurship

Before building anything, perform deep diligence into the potential customer (target market). Chapter 2 expands on this fundamental principle, which distills into developing a deep understanding of potential customers, challenges they want to solve or needs they want to address, and their willingness to pay for your solution.

Context for this reality is that entrepreneurs and all businesses ultimately work for their customers. Yes, entrepreneurship offers certain freedoms. And the source of those freedoms is a business that generates value, and as a result of earned relevance, revenue, by serving others.

As an entrepreneur, in essence, you are the first employee in service to a specific customer. Until someone pays for your offering, you don't have a business; you have a project or a hobby.

From Passion to Performance – What Do You Do Best?

As entrepreneurs, we tend to believe we need to be good at everything. And that belief may arise from necessity. Early in the journey, entrepreneurs wear every hat - product R&D, production, marketing, sales, finance, human resources - out of necessity.

As organizations grow, opportunities to share tasks with others – employees, partners, outsourced service providers – arise. A common limiting factor entrepreneurs experience is holding onto the "I have to do it all" mindset for too long.

When we're honest with ourselves, we can acknowledge that there are many things which are not our strengths. In fact, for most humans, our list of superpowers is shorter than the list of things that are not in our wheelhouse. The self-reflection question is not how to turn weaknesses into strengths, but to ask, what do I do uncommonly well? When we are clear with ourselves about our own strengths and superpowers we are prepared to make better decisions in translating ideas to business opportunities.

The Entrepreneur's Journey

These questions will help determine how to allocate activities to others in your entrepreneur journey:

- What are my greatest strengths and skills as a businessperson?
- What are my challenges and skills gaps?
- What skills should I seek from others to help advance this business?
- At what point can I outsource activities that are better performed by someone else?
- At what point should I hire someone in-house with the skills this business needs to advance?

The key is to optimize your role as entrepreneur around your highest-value contribution and design the business operating model to support that. The breadth and depth of the gig economy enable access to most skills a business needs on a contractor basis. Expertise in product design and prototyping, supply chain logistics, product manufacturing, marketing and social media, virtual assistants, human resource management, bookkeeping and accounting, and legal advice as outsourced or freelanced services have all developed meaningfully post-Covid, empowering entrepreneurs to spend more time doing what they do best. This operating model design approach comes into play at each level of growth, from solopreneur to a business with hundreds of employees.

One of my experiences with leveraging strengths was in my consulting practice. One Saturday, I was working on a client presentation and asked my son (at the time, a consultant with a large consulting firm) for help developing a particular slide for the deck. He is great at distilling complex data into meaningful graphics and was happy to help. When he finished the task, he said, "Dad, why are you wasting your time building this PowerPoint deck? There are other people who would do a much better job on this. And isn't your time better used helping your clients solve problems?" He was right. Even with powerful AI tools, it takes me much longer to create a PowerPoint deck than someone who excels in that skill, and it distracts me from where I add the most value to clients.

Closing Thoughts

The journey from idea to entrepreneurship requires due diligence into what the need I plan on addressing is, why your solution will be relevant (pertinent, meaningful, valuable to potential customers), and how you will bring the solution to fruition. This means developing a deep understanding of:

- **Alignment with your market**: knowing who you serve and what they value
- **Alignment with your strengths**: building your role around what you do best
- **Alignment with your resources**: filling in the gaps with the right people at the right time Knowing what you do best, how and when to delegate, outsource or insource activities to others based on their expertise

The best entrepreneurs are not usually lone geniuses. They are builders who combine clarity and focus with consistent execution. Your idea can become a business. But only when it's grounded in real customer demand, supported by your unique capabilities, and strengthened by a smart team strategy. Start with the foundation. Everything else grows from there.

The Entrepreneur's Journey

Chapter 2
Know your Customer and How to Serve Them

The Federal Reserve has a regulatory requirement for banks called Know Your Customer, or KYC. The purpose of KYC requirements is to ensure banks is understand who their customers are, the nature of their activities, and the risks they present.

In the entrepreneurial arena, knowing your customer is much more than a regulatory requirement. It is a business survival mandate. In the words of Peter Drucker, the purpose of a business is to create a customer. Drucker believed it is the customer who determines what a business is. How does one create a customer? Identify a need, satisfy it, monitor changes in the need, and adjust how you satisfy it. Drucker contextualized this principle with a set of questions for businesses to address:

- Who is your customer, the person (business, organization) you wish to satisfy with your offering?
- What does your customer value?
- What is your mission, in other words, what are you trying to accomplish for your customers?
- What results are you trying to accomplish?
- What is your plan? How do you go about satisfying your customers and getting the results that are most important?

The Entrepreneur's Journey

In *The Soul of Strategy: Building Customer Centric Organizations*, authors Bernard Jaworski and David Sprott take Drucker's principles further, defining Customer Centricity as an organization-wide effort to serve target market segments by making evidence-based market choices that create mutual value.

Jaworski and Sprott chose each word in this definition intentionally. Target market segments means businesses need to select and prioritize where they focus their resources, and that generally suggests one segment or a small number of intentionally chosen segments; they do not serve the entire market. Organization-Wide Effort says that customer centricity is not just a marketing endeavor; it is imbedded in every primary function of the organization's value chain, including how and where resources are allocated based on the customer. Evidence-Based Decisions are based on the voice of the marketplace (aka: the customer), not management's judgement or intuition. Market Choices include product offering (value proposition of your specific product), segment prioritization, shaping the market (not simply accepting current customer behavior as a given), and abandonment of products and activities no longer relevant to the market. Create Mutual Value says that the more relevant the business is to its customers through value creation, the more valuable the firm becomes.

Taken together, the principles of customer centricity guide us into a deep appreciation for the fullness of knowing your customer – who they are, what they value, what they're willing to pay for. Jaworski and Sprott write, "Customer-centric organizations are driven by unique, novel insights that can be deployed to create both customer and organizational value."

Defining Your Target Market: The Path to Clarity

When you understand the fundamentals of knowing your customer and the strategic foundation behind customer centricity, the next step in the entrepreneurial journey is to move from principle to practice. This begins with clearly defining who your customer is, with specificity that enables action. Broad categories like "small businesses," "working parents", or "tech-savvy Gen Z's" lack the granularity needed to create meaningful engagement, product development, and marketing strategies. Instead, defining your customer means identifying a specific segment of the market whose needs align most closely with the value you offer and who are willing to pay for that value.

Consider these steps to deepen clarity about the customer you serve:

Step 1: Clarify your customer segment.

Market segmentation is the process of dividing the broader market into smaller, manageable groups of individuals or organizations that share common characteristics, behaviors, or needs. These segments can be defined by:

Demographics: Age, income, gender, education, occupation.

Psychographics: Beliefs, values, lifestyle, personality traits.

Behavioral traits: Purchasing patterns, brand loyalty, usage frequency.

Geographic location: Urban vs. rural, region, climate, local culture.

Firmographics (for B2B): Industry type, company size, annual revenue, purchasing decision processes.

The goal is to identify which combination of these variables corresponds most directly with the customer who finds your offering not only relevant but essential.

Step 2: Understand what your customer will pay for.

Knowing your customer also means knowing what they truly value, and what they are willing to pay for. Entrepreneurs often fall into the trap of assuming value based on product features (remember the Juicero story), innovativeness of the product, or offering uniqueness, rather than through the lens of customers' perceived benefit. To avoid this, consider:

- What problem is your customer trying to solve or need do they want to address?
- How urgent or important is this problem to them?
- What alternatives are they currently using to address this need/problem, and what are the limitations of those alternatives?
- What tangible outcomes do they expect from a solution like yours?

This line of inquiry doesn't just clarify the value proposition; it also helps entrepreneurs understand pricing sensitivity. In many cases, customers aren't paying for the product or service itself, but for what it enables them to do better, faster, or more effectively.

Step 3: Validate Your Assumptions with Evidence.

As Jaworski and Sprott emphasize, customer-centricity is built on *evidence-based* decisions. Entrepreneurs must resist the temptation to build a business on untested assumptions or anecdotal insights. Evidence-based validation comes through deliberate methods like:

- Customer interviews, surveys, or focus groups to gather direct feedback from prospective customers in your target segment.
- Market testing by performing pilot programs, delivering prototypes, or minimum viable products (MVPs) to gauge customer responses and feedback.
- Sales data and usage metrics as quantitative evidence of how customers interact with your offering.

Each method helps refine your understanding of who you serve, what they value, and how well your offering aligns with their needs.

Step 4: Define the Target Customer Profile (TCP).

Once you've gathered enough insight, distill your findings into a clear Target Customer Profile. This is a concise representation of your most valuable customer, the one most likely to benefit from your offering, pay for it, and stay loyal over time. Your TCP should include:

- Who your customers are (demographic, psychographic, or firmographic characteristics)
- What they want (core needs or desired outcomes)
- Why they choose you (key differentiators, aka: your firm's value proposition)
- How they buy (decision-making process and buying behavior)

The Entrepreneur's Journey

This level of clarity helps inform optimal resource allocation decisions including product development, marketing, and sales, as well as where and how to expand.

Keep in mind - knowing your customer is an ongoing process, not an event. The process involves discovery, testing, and refinement as customer needs and expectations evolve. Entrepreneurs who invest in defining their customers and segments understand what those segments value and validate assumptions with evidence position themselves to build a more effective product and an agile, adaptive business.

Which Niche? Get Clear About how you Want to Play

It's said that in Hollywood, there are only a handful of basic movie plots: David and Goliath, rags to riches, quest, comedy, tragedy, rebirth. Characters, twists and turns, and the details vary, but every movie storyline is built from these basics. In the business world, we can say the same thing. The basic competitive strategy plotlines are low-price leadership, product innovation, differentiation, or niche player.

As with movie storylines, entrepreneurs choose a fundamental strategic approach to engaging customers, then build their business around the positioning. Here are some well-known, large company examples to illustrate the point:

- **Walmart**: Low-price leadership
- **Apple**: Product innovation
- **Chipotle**: Differentiation
- **Boeing Employees Credit Union:** Niche player

In his seminal book *Competitive Strategy: Techniques for Analyzing Industries and Competitors,* Michael Porter describes these foundational strategies (or basic movie plots) in the

Know Your Customer and How to Serve Them

context of an industry's competitive intensity, defined as the relative power of suppliers, level of threat from potential new industry participants, relative power of customers, level of threat from potential substitutes for the product or service, and the degree of competition among current industry participants.

With each strategy choice comes a set of supporting actions. A business competing as a low-price leader, for example, must apply its attention, resources, and objectives to driving costs as low as possible to succeed.

Product innovators, meanwhile, disproportionately invest in research and development to populate a pipeline of new, monetizable ideas.

Differentiators focus on what makes their offering unique and of value to customers.

Finally, niche players build and sustain competency and earn relevance with their specific, unique clientele. Niche players are also clear about who (which customer segments) they do not serve.

As an entrepreneur, whether in an early stage, scaling, or stuck at a plateau, there are essential questions to address about the positioning of your firm:

- Is our offering designed to serve a niche market? If so, how will we differentiate or compete with other players in the niche?
- If we are approaching the market as a product innovator, how will we sustain this positioning through our initial product offering and on an ongoing basis?
- If we are approaching the market as a low-cost leader, what scale/volume of production is necessary to compete with larger firms?

For every business, it is essential to know who your customers are, what they value, how to serve them, and to create the most impactful business model in context of a dynamic operating environment. For example, community (entrepreneurial) banks are either niche players or differentiators, not low-cost providers. Their customers tend to value personal relationships with a bank over higher deposit rates or lower loan rates. Some community banks have developed strong niche positions, like focusing on manufacturing equipment financing for small businesses (Beacon Bank in South Carolina), or military families and veterans (USAA Federal Savings Bank).

Occasionally, a community bank will deploy a strategy to pay high deposit rates to attract new deposit customers. The issue: strategic misalignment (operating like an industry low-cost leader when their economics are quite different than the megabanks). The result: Transitory deposits from non-customers who are always looking for the next best deal, and a distraction from strategies that better align with the community bank's competitive opportunities.

How to Define Your Competitive Strategy

Defining, designing, and deploying competitive strategy is like playing chess. It requires future thinking while building in the present moment. Analyzing the chess board involves considering potential consequences of each move, assessing risks and rewards, and determining the best course of action. The chess player considers their opponent's range of possible moves, strengths, and weaknesses, then plans responses several steps in advance. Successful chess players demonstrate agility, adapting mid-game strategies to respond to unexpected moves or unforeseen circumstances. Winning a chess game isn't just about making the best next move; it's about achieving a long-term objective. Both chess and entrepreneurs have finite resources - pieces in chess and capital (human, intellectual, physical, financial) in business. Making the most of these resources involves careful allocation and prioritization, focusing on high-impact activities that optimize return on investment.

As you consider setting your company's competitive chessboard, these actionable ideas will help affirm a competitive strategy that fits your business characteristics and competencies:

- **Get clear about your company's competencies and capacity.** Defining the best positioning for an entrepreneur's competitive strategy requires candid assessment of your available resources and scale (today and in the near-term), which combined represent capacity. Is your company's capacity aligned with low-volume production, high-volume, high value-add, or limited value-add? What are the organization's core competencies and how do they align with capacity? How will the company build on its competencies? How do your firm's competencies compare with those of your competitors, and how does this inform competitive positioning? Organizational competencies (like capturing continuous efficiency gains, innovativeness, distinctive customer engagement approach, natural niches) are opportunities to build upon and add color to your business's competitive positioning. These questions help determine how you solidify your competitive position.

- **Get clear about how you want to play the game.** Understand your target customers, your company's competencies and capacity, and the best way to compete. Is the company structured to be a low-price leader, or better aligned with differentiation? Is the firm a product innovator, always offering something new and engaging, or is it a better way to focus on a unique set of customer needs?

Candidly answering these questions helps set up the chess board for an engaging game.

The National Weather Service describes the Fujiwhara effect as an intense dance around the common center of two different hurricanes. The storms spin each other around for a while before moving off on their own paths, or they gravitate towards each other until they reach a common point and merge (aka: hurricane collision). Entrepreneurs that lack a clearly defined competitive strategy can lead a business into Fujiwhara-type conditions.

With an objective view into your company's best competitive strategy positioning, it is easy to identify activities that do not align. If the business has drifted into a danger zone (for instance, you find that new customers are only interested in low prices, but your operating costs don't support heavy discounts), it's time to do a competitive strategy alignment assessment. You may find activities that should be discontinued or refined to align with your foundational competitive strategy.

Chapter 3
Plan, Adjust, Repeat

At the first meeting with a new consulting client, I asked the CEO my standard opening questions: Tell me about your business, what is working well, what are some of the challenges you're facing, and what does success look like for the company. I was hired for this engagement by the company's board chair who was concerned about the CEO's effectiveness and her ability to adapt to changes taking place in their business.

The CEO talked about the company's thirty-year history, how their counselling service had grown from two therapists who started the practice, to a professional staff of fifty-five licensed marriage and family counsellors and PhDs across four locations. She started with the practice as a therapist, moved into management, then, two years before we met, was named CEO of the firm.

She shared the types of clients they serve, how they market their practice, and what it was like to manage her team. When I asked about the challenges, top of the list was navigating new regulatory complexities in the state for hiring professional therapists (contractors vs. employees), followed by adjusting to the post-Covid environment for serving clients.

Before going further, I asked about the firm's business plan. The CEO said they used the plan their founders developed when they launched the practice, but she wasn't sure where the document was located. That lead us to a fascinating conversation about how everything in the counselling business changed during Covid – the types of issues clients needed to address, frequency and nature of counselling sessions, therapists need for new training and changing their expectations of the firm, insurance parameters for counselling reimbursement, and the list went on.

At that point in the conversation, it was clear that this entrepreneurial firm was stuck in the past. Certainly, Covid accelerated the rate of change in their business, but over the twenty-five years prior to the pandemic, their business operating conditions were in perpetual motion. It was simply less obvious when the change velocity felt slower pre-pandemic.

What I thought, but didn't say, is "What do you expect? Business is in perpetual motion, but you are operating in the post-Covid world with a business plan designed for the Commodore 64 era (an early personal computer system in the 1980s)! I'm not surprised your board is concerned about the firm's agility." The points from this case: Planning is not a static one-and-done event. It is a dynamic, ongoing process, adjusted as business operating conditions evolve; and they always evolve.

From Vision to Action

As discussed in the Introduction chapter, every entrepreneur starts with a vision. As the ancient proverb says, vision without action is a daydream; action without vision is a nightmare. Entrepreneurs must build a navigable bridge between strategic themes and operational execution. This means translating your business idea, model, goals, and strategies into day-to-day execution.

Plan, Adjust, Repeat

Whether that vision is sketched on a napkin, like Herb Kellher's original business plan for Southwest Airlines, or laid out in a sleek pitch deck, it's the seed of something larger. At some point, the idea must be translated into a clear definition of success (aka: vision for the business) and a structured operating plan - something that bridges the gap between idea and execution.

When entrepreneurs contemplate their company's vision, it can feel ethereal or like wishful thinking instead of a substantive business exercise. Vision is the company's answer to the question: what does success look like for us? It's not esoteric or amorphous. It is simply how an organization defines success. While the path in a journey (strategy) is subject to continually evolving conditions, the destination (in the case of a business, the vision) generally remains fixed.

Meaningful, actionable vision statements are:

- Aspirational – Future-focused picture of how your business will contribute to the world.

- Inspirational – You and your team members feel motivated to play a role in bringing the vision to life.

- Meaningful – Each day, team members determine how to align their decisions and actions toward vision fulfilment.

Vision is a stable touchstone for execution of your business plan in an operating environment in perpetual motion. While customers, employees, competitors, and technology change, your company's vision remains stable. It provides context for people within the business to adapt to their changing operating environment.

These well-known company sample vision statements meet the aspirational, inspirational, and meaningful criteria:

- **Amazon**: To be Earth's most customer-centric company, Earth's best employer, and Earth's safest place to work.
- **Southwest Airlines:** To be the world's most loved, most efficient, and most profitable airline.
- **LEGO:** A global force of learning through play.
- **Zoom:** Communications empowering people to accomplish more.
- **Feeding America:** A hunger-free America.
- **Smithsonian:** Shaping the future by preserving our heritage, discovering new knowledge, and sharing our resources with the world.
- **TED**: Spread ideas.

One standard question I ask in consulting engagements is: How does your organization define success? Entrepreneurs often respond with sales goals, profitability metrics, or growth goals. These are all aspects of how a firm measures results, but not the definition of success, as the examples above illustrate.

Values are a business's core principles and beliefs that guide its priorities, actions, decisions, and define culture. When values synchronize with the company's vision, they create a strong sense of belonging for team members. Clearly defined value pillars put into words what the company cares about and inform appropriate organizational behavior; they also shine a bright light on misaligned activities and choices. This means entrepreneurs just paying lip service to stated values will appear inauthentic. Examples of value pillars are integrity, teamwork, diversity and inclusion, customer centricity, and contribution to the greater good.

Demonstrated values provide context to guide the company in navigating challenges and opportunities while remaining aligned with the vision. Because values create a sense of unity and purpose, they contribute to a feeling of stability in an environment in perpetual motion.

As an entrepreneur, you generally are involved in every aspect of running your business. That's why it is important to align your actions with the company's vision and values to guide people and priorities. Absent a clear vision, organizations, processes, and entrepreneurs inevitably drift from their goals. Without demonstrating a consistent set of values, employees can feel uncertain and unclear about what the company stands for. This is particularly true with startups and early-stage companies.

With a clear vision and values, businesses can find comfort in uncertainty, grounding through change, and stability in progress. In an environment where normal is continually redefined, stability and strategic resilience stem from alignment with the organization's vision and values.

Plan, Adjust. Repeat

It's easy to view planning as something to get done so you can move on to the real work. In reality, planning *is* the real work. It forces clarity, identifies priorities, uncovers blind spots, and lays the foundation for decision-making in times of uncertainty.

The Entrepreneur's Journey

From experience, I understand that for many entrepreneurs, the term *business plan* creates images of lengthy documents created for partners, investors, or banks, quickly filed away and rarely revisited. In reality, planning is not about a document, it's about discipline and creating a process that evolves with your business. Whether you're launching, scaling, or stuck at a frustrating plateau, businesses that thrive are not those with the most detailed plans, but those most adaptable over time.

A strong body of evidence shows that developing, implementing a business plan, and revisiting it as operating conditions change significantly improves an entrepreneur's outcomes. An analysis of forty-six studies on the value of business planning for established small and especially new firms, presented in the *Journal of Business Venturing*[1], found firms that prepare formal plans outperform otherwise similar non-planners. Another longitudinal study[2] covering 223 Swedish startups goes further, suggesting planning helps founders sequence critical actions, balance resources, accelerate product development, and lowers the risk of disbanding as benefits tied to actually using the plan.

For entrepreneurs, the message is clear: For those startups and early-stage companies who develop and deploy plans are measurably more likely to achieve viability. For established companies, the advantage compounds when plans are updated and resources are reallocated to address current priorities. Businesses that actively and regularly refresh plans and shift capital create more value and deliver higher shareholder

---

[1] https:www.sciencedirect.com/science/article/abs/pii/S0883902608
[2] https://sms.onlinelibrary.wiley.com/doi/abs/10.1002.smj.349?utm source=chatgpt.com

Plan, Adjust, Repeat

returns than those that stick to static, once-a-year planning (McKinsey & Company)[3].

An entrepreneur's business plan is not intended to predict every detail. It is a strategic GPS that guides your company's direction even as conditions change (and they always change).

Business Plan Basics

In the spirit of Coach Wooden walking his team members through the fundamentals with each new basketball season, it is time to cover the basics of a living, breathing business plan. If you have that moment reading through this when you say, "I already know all this," great! If the information is new, that's great too.

What Is a Business Plan?

A business plan is a clear, organized document that explains what your business does, who your customer is and how you will serve them, and describes your go-to-market strategy. It serves as a roadmap for launching, managing, and expanding your business. Where do you begin the plan development process?

Start with the customer and your vision. As discussed in the Know You're your Customer chapter, this element of planning begins with a clear description of who you serve, the problem you will solve, or need you will address, and what your customer values.

---

[3] https://www.mckinsey.com/capabilities/strategy and corporate science/our-insights/how nimble-resource-allocation-can-double-your companys-value?utm_source+chatgpt.com

The Entrepreneur's Journey

From your customer description you can define your company's target market. For entrepreneurs, the Serviceable Obtainable Market is key. Total Addressable Market (TAM) is the entire market demand for your type of product or service. Serviceable Available Market (SAM) is the segment of TAM that your business can realistically reach with its current offerings and distribution. That distills to the portion of SAM that you can realistically capture in the near-to-medium term – the SOM (Serviceable Obtainable Market).

A clear understanding of your SOM informs your initial business model definition in terms of revenue potential, how to enter or develop the market, and how to position your offering in contrast to existing competitors (if any exist). And knowing who your company serves informs a concise definition of success – your vision.

Describe your business model. Determine how you will serve your customer. Business models are discussed in detail in the next chapter. In context of business plan basics, an entrepreneur's business model (aka: go-to-market model or business operating model) is the way your company goes to market, or *how* each piece of the business fits together to serve customers. Your business model covers each key component, process, and resource necessary to create the desired outcomes. It guides decision-making and ensures team members' alignment with the company's vision.

Questions to help inform your business model include: What economic model will you deploy (target revenue volume, pricing strategy, profit margin targets)? If you produce a physical product, will you outsource manufacturing or do it yourself? What supply chain approach will you take? Will you differentiate your offering through a unique customer experience? Will you distribute directly, or through agents, online, or independent retailers? How will you engage with your customers or distributors (in person, online, both)? How will you ensure long-term, repeat customers? What will your ongoing customer relationship management approach be? What pricing strategy will you offer?

The business model is core to your plan. It connects your vision to priorities and daily actions.

Business Plan Elements

- Executive Summary - A brief snapshot of your business, including vision (how you define success), offering, and success measures.
- Business Description – Who you serve, how you serve your customers, vision, go-to-market model, objectives, and legal structure.
- Market Analysis – Describe your TAM, SAM, and SOM, insights into your industry, competitive characteristics, and market trends.
- Products or Services - What you are providing, what makes it unique, and any intellectual property involved.
- Marketing & Sales - How you plan to attract and retain customers, including pricing and promotion strategies.
- Operations & Management - The team, organizational structure, and how day-to-day activities will be managed.
- Financial Projections – Revenue forecasts, expenses, cash flow, and profits over the plan period.

- Risk Management - Key risks and how you plan to mitigate and manage them.

The Myth of the "Set-It-and-Forget-It" Plan

The opening story of this chapter illustrates a common planning mistake - developing a plan *once* and never looking at it again. Business planning is not an event; it's a continuous process. Markets and industries change. Customers evolve. Competitors adapt. What worked well last year may no longer apply. Entrepreneurs who treat their plan as static risk falling out of sync with reality.

The most effective business plans are dynamic. They're reviewed regularly. Adjusted when needed, and preemptively when new opportunities arise. Plans are used as a living tool to steer the business forward, not just backward-looking documentation.

For early-stage founders, this might involve setting 90-day goals and defining simple Key Performance Indicators. For scaling businesses, it often means introducing a regular planning cadence - monthly reviews, quarterly goal-adjustments, and annual strategic refreshes. The point is not to build complexity, but to establish rhythm for plan review, refresh, and business model updates.

What is the Shelf Life of Your Business Plan?

The concept of "normal" business conditions is frequently misunderstood to mean static. Nothing could be further from reality. The nature of business is perpetual motion as customers, employees, competitors, regulations, economic conditions, and every other variable in the operating environment evolve.

Entrepreneurs must recognize the need for unceasingly redefining normal and building on this reality to guide your business in earning and sustaining relevance - pertinence, meaningfulness, importance - with employees, customers, and all stakeholders. Entrepreneurs need to ask, "What comes next for this business, and what will it take for our company to earn and sustain relevance with our stakeholders tomorrow?"

The next phase of normal is a constantly evolving story for each business to write, beginning now. But, if normal is in flux, where can entrepreneurs find stability? In the business world, the answer lies in your company's vision, values, and business plan, which guide people and priorities and informs strategy execution when the definition of normal is in perpetual motion. This means your business plan is a dynamic document, reviewed and refined frequently.

Plan Reviews vs. Financial Reviews

Business plan operating reviews are often confused with financial performance reviews. These are two different things. The bottom-line matters. The key question: What is the right bottom line for your business?

There is nothing wrong with using metrics to evaluate outcomes. Financial analysis is essential for entrepreneurs in diagnosing operating results. But the bigger question is: what activities (or lack thereof) created the conditions reflected in your financial results?

Mastering your metrics means knowing which measures best reflect *root causes* of operating results. For instance, *profit margin* reflects the business's cost of delivering its offering to customers at a point in time in context of pricing decisions; total revenue earned from customer purchases, less total costs. On its own, profit margin tells only the cost of generating revenue. It does little at the surface level for answering "why" questions about results.

In a sense, traditional financial performance metrics like profit margin are blunt instruments when it comes to answering "why" questions. Greater meaning for entrepreneurs comes from understanding what *caused* customers to buy what you're selling, and how effectively you applied your resources to deliver your offering. On the revenue front, metrics to master emanate from *relevan*ce– the level of pertinence, meaningfulness, importance customers ascribe to your offering.

Focusing on the right bottom line informs entrepreneurs about which activities have the greatest impact on outcomes. This enables you to enhance operating efficiency, with the goal of earning and sustaining relevance to customers.

Rather than making a case for a target efficiency ratio or pretax profit margin as the goal, this approach helps answer the question: How are we serving our customers? The "how" touches on things like effective resource allocation, pricing strategy, and relationship value, all toward the purpose of earning and sustaining relevance with your customers. Looking below the surface leads to deeper understanding and new ideas to fulfill the organization's vision.

When Relevance is at Risk, Refine Your Plan

What can entrepreneurs do when earning or sustaining relevance with customers is at risk? This is time for a business plan review. Step one is to deconstruct operating activities to ensure alignment with your company's vision and existing plan. Revisiting fundamental questions like who your target customer is, how you are serving them, are customers' expectations changing, do you understand what they want and are willing to pay for, and are you serving the right customers is essential to the business plan review process, and helps surface issues requiring attention.

In *Islands of Profit in a Sea of Red Ink*, MIT lecturer, Jonathan Byrnes wrote – "Nearly 40% of every company's activities are unprofitable by any measure, and 20% to 30% are so profitable that they provide all the reported earnings, thereby cross-subsidizing losses. The rest of the company is only marginally profitable." The most frequent root cause? Serving the *wrong* customer. Earning relevance, ergo revenue, with customers your business model isn't designed to serve is a losing proposition.

The Feedback Loop: Assess, Adapt, Advance

Effective planning includes a consistent feedback loop. Entrepreneurs should get into the habit of asking:
- What's working?
- What's underperforming?
- Where are we off course?
- What new opportunities are emerging?

For startups, this may be a weekly founder check-in. For growing teams, a monthly review involving team leaders may be more effective. The cadence matters less than the consistency of reflection.

The Entrepreneur's Journey

Getting unstuck and Adaptive Disruptive conversations

My daughter worked in a boutique men's shoe store in New York's West Village. One cold, rainy day, a woman frantically entered the store. Very upset, she shrieked, "I need your help! My left foot is stuck inside my rainboot, and I've tried everything, but can't pull it off. I just went to the fire station across the street, and the chief said they couldn't help me. I looked at your sign and see that you're a shoe store, and I'm hoping you can help me get unstuck!"

My daughter said, "Removing stuck boots isn't really what we do here, but we'll try to help you. Just have a seat and we'll see what we can do." A co-worker put her arms around the woman's abdomen to hold her in the seat, then my daughter grabbed hold of the rainboot at the heel and began pulling.

Finally, after a few failed attempts, the stuck rainboot came off. The woman was relieved and quite grateful.

She said, "If you girls didn't help me get unstuck, I don't know what I would have done!"

She stood up, turned toward the shoe store door, then put the rainboot right back on her left foot. Stuck, unstuck, then stuck again.

This story is a metaphor for a condition entrepreneurs often experience. We often invest a lot of time and energy in getting "unstuck" from conditions that don't help advance our business. Then when we get unstuck, we step right back into the same suboptimal conditions again. Often, we get stuck because the operating environment has changed. Competition has shifted, new offerings are available to our customers, or customer expectations have shifted.

Plan, Adjust, Repeat

In my book, *Leading from Zero: Seven Essential Elements of Earning Relevance*, I discuss the notion of Adaptive Disruption. The adaptive disruption principle posits that entrepreneurs can effectively interpret competitive threats as clues that customers' needs, interests, and values may be changing. Rather than study what disruptors do, we go to the source – our customers – to deepen our understanding of what matters to them here and now. We revisit those fundamental questions: *What do our customers want? Are their needs changing? Are we prepared to adapt to unfolding customer needs?* and *How do our firm's competencies lend themselves to addressing recognized and unrecognized needs?*

Asymmetrical disruptors are prevalent in most industries. Therefore, we must assume barriers to entry in an industry are perishable or are easily overcome, potential for new competitors is high, competitive advantages are temporary, and pricing pressure is constant. Within this context, the Adaptive Disruption approach takes ownership of activities within the organization's control and navigates those which are not to fulfil the vision. Stimulus is external; response is internal and aligned with the company's vision. Remaining aligned with the vision requires strategic conversation and contemplation to shape effective actions as disruption surfaces.

Conversation #1 – *Does our vision still fit the organization?*

Vision is the future state and defines the organization's place in the world. It combines mission, purpose, and strategy. Vision connects what your organization does through its competencies to the external world.

As clues of emerging disruption and paradigm shift sprout up, revisiting the vision guides leaders through alignment assessment. While vision is enduring, it must be adaptive to ensure the organization earns and sustains relevance. Adaptive Disruption strategy opens the door to refining vision, if necessary, to earn relevance. It also helps entrepreneurs who are stuck at an operating plateau recalibrate.

A common entrepreneurial mistake is reacting to emerging paradigm shifts starting with financial decisions. Evidence of impending disruption causes a Pavlovian response to recast financial expectations, cut costs, or eliminate functions. These are not inherently poor actions, merely the wrong initial response to a changing environment. Numbers measure results, not why a business exists. Starting with the vision enables entrepreneurs to focus on root cause, not effect.

Conversation #2 – *All things considered, what strategic priorities will enhance the relevance of our business?*

Considering the disruptive indicators we're observing, what are the most important two or three strategic priorities to deliver beyond expected financial results over the next 36 months to enhance relevance with employees, customers, and stakeholders?

What prioritized activities should the business engage in to fulfill its vision? With a clear future state picture, the firm prepares to translate its reaffirmed vision into refined priorities supporting an Adaptive Disruption strategy. Now the future state picture becomes actionable.

I read an article about the resurgence of something called Paint-by-Numbers. The idea came about in the 1950's as a mix between a coloring book and painting on a canvass. By starting with a clear picture of the desired result (future state), then following a step-by-step framework, anyone can create something beautiful.

Bringing vision to life is similar; it is irrelevant unless it informs priorities, and those priorities define actions: painting-by-numbers.

Conversation #3 - *How well do our actions align with our company's vision?*

Vision Drift is losing sight of the future state and, as a result, fragmenting attention, and distracting company resources. Close alignment creates better results. These questions help frame this conversation:

- Which of the activities we engage today in are most closely aligned with our vision?
- Which of the activities we engage in today are out of alignment with the vision?
- How are we assured our team members engage in activities most closely aligned with our vision?
- As a leader, how effectively do I address activities taking place in the business that don't appear to align with the vision?

Adaptive Disruption as an intentional strategy empowers entrepreneurs to earn and re-earn relevance with stakeholders while driving continual evolution of the business toward manifesting the vision.

Embracing Iteration Over Perfection

It's tempting to wait until a business plan feels perfect before launching or scaling. A better approach is to start with a clear, flexible framework, launch with a clear vision and business priorities, gather data, and iterate based on results.

The Entrepreneur's Journey

Think of your business plan as a prototype—it should improve over time as you learn more about your customers, your team, and your market.

Planning isn't about knowing the future; it's about being prepared to meet it head-on.

Chapter 4
Go to Market Model Management

"Within five years, if you're in the same business you are in now, you're going to be out of business." — Peter Drucker

Imagine New Year's Eve, three years from now. While you're getting ready to ring in the new year with family and friends, you take a few minutes and reflect on the year now ending. As you think back over the past 12 months, a question comes to mind: *What did I do as a leader that had the greatest impact on my business this year?* Leading operating reviews? Developing new products? Analyzing financial performance? Coaching my direct reports? Recruiting new talent? Each of these activities matters, but their impact will be suboptimal if your business model is stale.

Every business operating model has a finite shelf-life, which at some point loses effectiveness as, over time, the operating environment changes. It's easy to see with examples like Blockbuster Video. Customer expectations for video content shifted from physical, retail store access to on-demand and eventually streaming. Alternative content delivery options, formats, and providers (Netflix, Amazon Prime Video, Hulu, Disney+ to name a few) became available. Then a global pandemic created an extraordinary accelerant in the evolution of entertainment content access. Changes in demand, supply, technology. and customer delivery alternatives all advanced the obsolescence of the retail video store business operating model.

Operating Conditions in Perpetual Motion

Perhaps it's more challenging to see similar shifts to operating model dynamics in your business, but conditions are in motion right now.

In 1979, Harvard Business School strategy professor Michael Porter wrote about how competitive forces shape strategy[4]. Porter discussed five competitive forces that define the attractiveness (relative competitiveness) of an industry: the threat of substitute products or services, threat of established rivals, threat of new entrants (contextualized with barriers to entry), bargaining power of suppliers, and bargaining power of customers. Prevailing wisdom says when barriers to entry are low in an industry, the risk of new companies venturing into a given market is high. Conversely, when barriers to entry are high (e.g. significant capital requirements to participate in the industry), incumbents have an advantage over new entrants.

Today, industry disruption is aided by technology and new approaches to innovation, which recalibrate these competitive forces. Most industries - including those once perceived to present high barriers to entry - are vulnerable to disruption. Innovators reduce time-to-market, elevating the threat of substitute offerings. In many industries, the hurdles of high upfront capital requirements no longer exist. E-commerce redefined the bargaining power of suppliers and customers and opened the door to a plethora of new business models.

---

[4] https://hbr.org/1979/03/how-competitive-forces-shape-strategy

Go to Market Model Management

Consider businesses associated with recorded music. The first-generation operating model for recording music dates to 1877, with Thomas Edison's invention of the phonograph. Early recording equipment captured sound on tin foil cylinders. Recording took place outdoors, in home workshops, or hotel rooms. Over the next two decades, technology advanced from Edison's initial inventions to disc-based gramophone and magnetic tape-recording devices.

As tools of the trade developed, professional recording studios designed to capture and transform sound evolved. By the 1950s, studios had become cutting edge, high-tech environments with the development of innovative recording techniques like multi-track recording and tape loops augmenting musical artists' creativity.

To advance and apply these technological developments, record companies and related businesses invested millions of dollars on acoustic design for sound studios, recording equipment and professional talent to engineer recordings. Studios like Abbey Road in London, Capitol Records in Los Angeles, and RCA Studios in Nashville became industry leaders, hosting iconic artists like The Beatles, Frank Sinatra, and Elvis Presley.

Further in the value chain, record producers worked with manufacturing firms, which required large capital investments in pressing and packaging equipment, physical distribution channels, and marketing resources.

The business model evolved to the point that due to high production costs, record companies would only invest in artists with a strong sales history. The cost-benefit of taking on new artists was so great that it limited exposure to new music from independent musicians.

The model was successful and effective until it wasn't. In the 1980s, digital recording technology came of age. Digital audio workstations replaced analog tape machines, enabling greater flexibility, editing capabilities, and affordability. In 1991, Pro Tools, an easy to use, low capital investment (originally around $6,000) digital workstation entered the market and transformed the recording process. Pro Tools enabled new, independent artists (not yet signed with a record label), to record their original music at home with studio-comparable quality.

Technology evolution, combined with the ability to distribute music through streaming platforms like Apple Music or Spotify and to market through social media is the foundation for an operating model where indie artists can compete with established musicians operating under a stale business model. Artists create and distribute their product directly to their audience, bypassing the legacy record company operating model.

When has a business model outlived its shelf life? When it no longer advances the organization in the direction of its vision. Identifying cues that conditions are in motion prepares leaders to take preemptive steps in model refinement before it loses relevance.

What is a Business Operating Model?

A firm's business model (aka: go-to-market model or business operating model) is the way the company goes to market. Business model and strategy are not synonymous. The business model shows how strategy is operationalized to serve customers in context of the macro environment. A business model describes *how* each piece of a business fits together to serve clients. The business model is fulfilment of strategy, which is distilled from demand, supply, and the competitive environment. Strategy guides development of the operating model.

The business operating model looks at each key component, process, and resource necessary to create the desired outcomes. It serves as a playbook for how the business operates, guiding decision-making and ensuring team members alignment with the organization's vision.

Each industry and business are unique. Still, there are common characteristics of a business operating model:

- **Target Customers and Specific Segments** (covered in detail in the Know Your Customer chapter) – Who the business serves (through inference, this also describes out-of-target customers), what the customer values, and what they will pay for. The more specific, the better.
- **Customer Engagement Approach** – How the organization connects to deliver its value proposition to its customers. Business-to-business, business-to-consumer, business-to-business-to-consumer, high touch, high tech, digital only.
- **Value Proposition** – Answers the customer's question: "Why should I choose your offering?" Describes how the business differentiates itself from competitors.
- **Activities and Process Design** – Defines core activities and processes necessary to deliver the value proposition and how they will be performed (i.e., what are the

organization's core competencies and which activities are better left to other firms, what will be produced in-house vs. outsourced or partner-supplied, what are optimal process workflows for efficiency and effectiveness).
- **Resources** – Defines essential resources required to operate the business, including capital, technology, physical assets, partnerships, and vendors.
- **Economic Model** – Describes costs associated with operating the business and informs marketplace positioning (i.e., low-cost leader, premium offering) and pricing strategy.
- **Talent Approach** – Are team members continually developed, effectively coached, properly managed, and thoroughly engaged? Does the company take a different approach to its employees?

Business Model Management

Some firms operate intentionally designed, consistently executed go-to-market business models. Others evolve models in a less structured manner. Regardless of genesis, changes across any of these seven characteristics suggest the need to review and refine a company's business operating model.

These seven steps guide entrepreneurs in business model development and refinement over time. Since business models have a finite shelf life, regular review and refinement in alignment with these steps is essential to long-term success:
- **Affirm (reaffirm) the business's definition of success (the company's vision)** – A company's vision is relatively stable, rarely changing. In a review of a

company's business model, it's essential to ask: Has our definition of success changed, and if so, how? Significant gaps between an existing vision and the business operating model suggests the company experienced scope creep or the vision needs refinement to reflect the focus of activities.

- **Affirm (re-affirm) the company's culture pillars** - Culture is the shared set of values, beliefs, and behaviors that characterize an organization and influence how its members interact with each other and their stakeholders. Pillars are those foundational descriptors describing the culture like integrity, teamwork, diversity and inclusion, customer centricity, and contribution to the greater good. Clearly defined and documented culture pillars help transmit and reinforce values aligned with vision.
- **Establish (re-establish) business priorities aligned with achieving the vision** – This short list of themes governs allocation of resources, time, and energy. As leaders consider establishing a priority, a first question is: How would this priority help advance our organization towards the vision? By ranking priorities high, medium, or low alignment with the stated vision, leaders can focus their resources where they will experience the greatest return. Conversely, if a proposed activity is outside the priorities, leaders must question investing and pay attention to it.
- **Distill priority-linked strategies** - Each priority is operationalized with specific strategies. By building

strategies in support of priorities that fulfil the vision, the company's daily activities are efficient.
- **Define and document refined operating model** - Includes specifics about Target Customers and Specific Segments, Customer Engagement Approach, Value Proposition, Activities and Process Design, Resources, Economic Model and Talent Approach.
- **Implement refined operating model** – Each element of the new operating model is allocated to the appropriate team or individual and distilled into individual performance expectations and metrics.
- **Facilitate ongoing change leadership** – Change leadership is not a stand-alone activity, rather it is simply a characteristic of leadership. As an element of business model development, this step can lead back to the first – Affirm the organization's vision as new change stimuli emerge.

Like managing any other organizational asset, business model management is an ongoing process requiring an entrepreneur's time and attention. When approached as a business-as-usual endeavor, all participants in the process are better positioned to navigate perpetual motion in the business operating environment.

Value of Self-Initiated Business Model Disruption

Abraham Lincoln once said, *"Things may come to those who wait, but only the things left by those who hustle."* Translated for business, this message may be interpreted to mean entrepreneurs can either act preemptively or reactively. If only the decision was so simple.

I participated in a series of fintech startup investor presentations. These early-stage companies sought venture capital funding to take their ideas to the next level of commercialization. By the fifth presentation, I heard the term "disruption" so many times, it sounded like an obligatory disclaimer: "Our goal is to disrupt the [fill-in-the-blank] industry." One could interpret the term as though it is a strategy in-and-of-itself; it is not.

It's easy to think of rapidly changing business environments such as those driven by technological development (like the fintech disruptors I observed) and new market entrants. But dynamic conditions are present in every area of business. A recent article in Funeral Director Daily[5] read, "As our environment continues to experience frequent change, safeguarding your business by remaining vigilant and adapting to the world around you is becoming increasingly important. Funeral Homes are now having to contend with an unpredictable economic climate, regular staff shortages and quickly changing consumer needs. Digitalization is also becoming a bigger part of the industry; digital guests are interacting with services in unique but impactful ways. Those who remain flexible unlock unique opportunities while avoiding the potential hardships that come with inactivity." No business or business model is immune to rapidly changing operating conditions, not even the funeral business.

Disruption happens. It's a natural force as industries evolve. John F. Kennedy said, "Change is the law of life. And those who

---

[5] https://funeraldirectordaily.com/adapting-to-change-in-2023/

look only to the past or present are certain to miss the future." Innovators capitalize on change to address evolving customer needs, interests, and preferences, and at the same time, many businesses let change take them by surprise.

Knowing the dynamic nature of business and the continuous redefinition of "normal," leaders have a decision to make - initiate change and innovation or react to external pressures forcing adjustment. The most effective leaders proactively look for every opportunity to preemptively refine business operating models and processes, increase efficiency, and improve products and services to their customers.

By practicing self-initiated disruption, entrepreneurs proactively identify opportunities to create a business model shift for the benefit of their organization's stakeholders. Austrian economist Joseph Schumpeter used the term "creative destruction" to describe the way free markets evolve. Drawing from Schumpeter's words, self-initiated disruption revolutionizes a business's value product (what it produces) from within, destroying the old one in favor of a new, more impactful value product.

Self-initiated business model disruption serves two purposes. First, it preempts external disruption by existing competitors and new entrants to your business. Second, it grounds the organization in its reason for existing through the employees, customers and stakeholders served.

Self-initiated disruption is an intentional strategy. Identification of opportunities for self-initiated disruption is a powerful tool for sustaining relevance through business model refinement and redesign.

Change is happening in your business right now. Why not step into *change leadership* through preemptive, self-initiated disruption and define the next iteration of your company's business operating model beginning today?

Defining Problems vs. Delivering Strategy

Entrepreneurs often fall into the trap of believing that if they can eliminate the company's problems, everything will be fine. They get mired in issue identification to the detriment of understanding how the operating environment changes and what those changes mean to their organization. More to the point, the tendency to overemphasize defining problems distracts attention from meaningful, actionable strategy work leading to business model refinement.

Strategic management is an entrepreneur's responsibility. It is an ongoing, dynamic process, comprised of leading your business for today, tomorrow, and beyond. Today's issues need resolution. The question is: How does the issue de jour become a benefit to our business? When contextualized relative to the company's long-term vision, issues can become connection points between today's actions (including problem resolution) and tomorrow's results.

How can entrepreneurs use business issues as strategic building blocks to move their organizations forward? Here are four pivots to help move a business from defining problems to strategic management:

Pivot 1: From eliminating pain points to a strategic management mindset

I worked with a bank CEO to organize a strategic planning session with his leadership team. When I asked what success looked like for the session, he held up his list of the top ten pain points his managers wanted to resolve. For him, at first blush, success was fixing things that caused his team and customers pain.

Focusing on removing pain points is a common but misplaced focus. There is nothing wrong with fixing things, but removing pain only gets the business to pain-free, not success. Success means performing activities aligned with the company's vision — moving toward something intentionally defined, not away from something that doesn't work.

The clearer a company is about what it is moving toward, the more successful it will be in executing its strategy. No successful company has a vision of simply being pain-free. There's more to success than the absence of issues. However, used properly, problems (or pain points) can bring clarity to a business's definition of success.

Pivot 2: From description to root cause

Businesspeople often dwell on describing problems in detail, followed by exhaustive analysis. This is particularly true when our business seems to be stuck at a plateau. Understanding a problem becomes relevant when leaders go beyond definition to root cause.

By getting to the root cause of an issue (disappointing financial results, declining employee engagement measures, or customer departures as examples), the problem can inform a pivot to the right set of actions that will create the desired outcomes.

Earning, re-earning, and sustaining relevance with customers and other stakeholders is a daily endeavor which requires a clear understanding of operating results - why a strategy works or falls short of producing expected outcomes. Deconstructing results and finding the root cause simply means understanding the set of activities and circumstances that created outcomes, then adjusting accordingly for different results.

Understanding the root cause leads to greater awareness and new ideas to fulfill the organization's vision.

Pivot 3: From struggle to strength

An effective business strategy and operating model emphasizes attention to core competencies - things a company does best - and steers clear of anything outside that nucleus. This means leaders must be honest with themselves and their organization about what their company does well and what would be better left to others.

Struggle is often an effect of engaging in activities, projects, or strategies that do not play to the company's strengths. There is tremendous power in knowing what your company doesn't do well or shouldn't do at all. When a business is clear in its future-state vision, it's easier to know which activities, decisions, hiring choices, or partnerships align - and which are out of scope.

Having this clarity helps avoid wasting time on activities that will never be a good fit with the business operating model. This applies to the daily activities a business invests its time in, as well as bigger-picture endeavors like joint ventures or mergers and acquisitions.

In-N-Out Burger[6] is a terrific example of playing to strengths. They make burgers, fries, and shakes. No chicken sandwiches. No veggie burgers. No salads. They do burgers, fries, and shakes exceptionally well (in the view of their customers, which is what counts).

Pivot 4: From issue identification to refined business model

There is power in problems when entrepreneurs leverage learnings from issue assessment to evolve a new business operating model. Business model longevity is defined by many variables described in this book. The sooner cues and clues which suggest it's time for a model refresh are examined, the better positioned the organization to advance toward its vision.

Back to New Year's Eve three years from now, and the self-imposed question: *What did I do as a leader that had the greatest impact on my business in over the past year?* One powerful answer can be, "Over the summer, I reviewed our company's business operating model and see how it aligns with the future we anticipate. The changes we made later that year led to a breakout performance and outstanding results!"

The Most Common Business Model Issues

It depends. I'm not sure exactly what it depends on, but I know – it depends. I'm referring to pizza. Homemade is my favorite, but when that's not an option and my wife and I don't

---

[6] https://digitalsparkmarketing.com/competitive-strategy/

want to go out for dinner, I'm happy to order home delivery pizza.

We usually order pizza from a local franchisee of a national chain. One Friday evening, Norma delivered our pizza. About half the time, she not only takes our phone order, but she makes the pizza and delivers it. On this particular night, Norma did it all – took our order, made the pizza, then delivered it.

When I saw her pull up in front of our house, I went out to the curb to meet her. Norma handed me the pizza, I thanked her, then turned around to go inside. As I headed back into the house, a neighbor passed by. She saw me carrying the pizza boxes and asked, "How do you like that pizza place?"

I felt the urge to respond immediately and say, "Norma is terrific, and she makes great pizzas." But I paused for a moment and thought - when Norma doesn't make the pizza, the product is inconsistent. Sometimes it's good; other times, it's not good at all. Not enough sauce, too little cheese, burned crust. My answer to the neighbor: "It depends."

I learned later (from Norma) that the pizza store has one process to fulfill online orders. Phone orders are handled differently, and walk-in orders receive a third approach. What does the customer get? It depends.

In contrast, Forklore Restaurant Group (pseudonym for an actual restaurant chain) is unwilling to accept "It depends" as a customer experience option. Forklore operates upscale restaurants under more than a dozen different brand names through a consistent business model. In the late 1970s, Forklore's founders set out to establish an upscale restaurant that combined consistency and quality in a manner not previously delivered in full-service restaurants. Forklore's commitment to create a consistent, repeatable dining experience was measured against a set of high standards and attention to details.

My introduction to Forklore Restaurant Group was through a restaurateur and founder of another large restaurant chain.

I asked, "When you're not eating at one of your restaurants, what is your favorite place to dine?"

He said, "Forklore in Newport Beach."

I asked, "Why?"

He said, "Consistency and quality."

Subsequently, I learned that Forklore restaurants train employees to deliver a consistent, engaging customer experience. Each step – from initial guest greeting, through delivery of first round beverages within two minutes of seating, how orders are taken, presentation of food for optimal aesthetics, check delivery, and everything in between – is thoroughly choreographed. Activities in the kitchen follow an equally well-defined operating model to assure food quality consistency. And managers ensure consistent end-to-end execution of the operating model.

Most restaurants want consistency for the guests. Forklore Restaurant Group deploys a business operating model that assures this.

When the answer is - It depends - there may be a business model issue at play. Evidence from the pizza store example suggests at least three different operating models, defined by ordering channel (phone, online, in-store), each with a different outcome. This is one of many common go-to-market business operating model issues.

Go to Market Model Management

Think about your experience as a customer or even as an employee of an organization with a poorly designed business model or no intentional model at all. When the answer is "It depends," outcomes are unpredictable, and as a result, business is at risk. In this chapter, we cover some of the most common business model issues.

No Clear Go to Market Model

Sometimes businesses grow out of a successful product or service. There is demand for the offering, which provides the producer with an initial engagement approach with the customer. In the software arena, a similar concept is the Minimum Viable Product which describes the basic version of a product with the minimum features needed to meet user needs. However, a product or service on its own is not a go-to-market business model.

When a well-defined go to market model has not been developed, or the model exists but is outdated, a company is likely to experience below average growth, increasing customer attrition, and economic challenges over time.

Recommended Action: Follow the seven-step approach to business model development described above to formalize a go-to-market model for your company or to assess an existing model you suspect may be outdated.

Unclear or Undeveloped Playbook

Imagine attending a Broadway musical which had no script, no choreography, no blocking. Actors are left to their own creativity to tell the story, develop, and deliver their lines, sing their songs, and interact with other performers. Odds are the audience would see confusion, disorganization, or chaos on stage.

In contrast, Broadway plays generally have thoroughly developed scripts, performed by highly trained actors who have memorized their lines, learned the choreography, and know exactly how to engage with their colleagues on stage.

When a firm has not developed a playbook for serving customers, the result can look like the play without a script. Leaders and staff do their best to deliver to customers, but performances are improvised and inconsistent.

A well-defined playbook serves as a roadmap that outlines the firm's approach to customer engagement. Team choreography and customer experience are defined, roles and responsibilities are clear, and management can focus on consistent execution.

Recommended Action: After defining your business model, develop a playbook to describe roles, responsibilities, and outcomes for your business. Rather than a document for occasional reference, this playbook becomes the roadmap for all team members.

Lack of a Clearly Defined Target Customer or Specific Segments

Who is our customer? This is a simple question that often goes unanswered or is answered in a manner incongruent with the business. Yet failure to define your customer can have significant economic and resource allocation implications.

I worked with an independent wealth management firm that had 9,500 accounts for 4,000 clients (most clients have multiple accounts). Our engagement focused on the

Go to Market Model Management

identification of opportunities to accelerate growth. Through our discovery and assessment process, we learned staffing was the top growth constraint.

On further analysis, a more profound issue arose. While the company had a stated minimum relationship size of $500,000 (value of all assets managed for a client across accounts), the actual average relationship size was below $200,000. That meant a business model designed for larger relationships – defined as clients with at least $500,000 managed by the firm – overloaded its resources. It takes two and a half $200,000 relationships to equal one $500,000 relationship. A staffing model developed to handle larger relationships was choked with more than twice the volume people were prepared to service.

The solution to this firm's business model issue was two-fold – re-establish clarity about their target client and develop a segmentation strategy to effectively serve existing smaller relationships. Through this exercise, the firm increased its minimum new relationship size to $1 million in managed assets.

Recommended Action: As discussed in the Know Your Customer chapter, define your business's target customer. Your target customer should be one you can serve exceptionally well, drawing from the company's core competencies. If your customer base is large, explore segmentation and provide differentiated offerings in each segment served as economically warranted.

Inconsistent or Poorly Defined Customer Experience (aka Customer Engagement)

"If you don't know where you are going, any road can take you there." Those words from *Alice in Wonderland*'s Cheshire Cat work in a children's storybook. Lacking a clear destination in the customer journey doesn't work so well.

When each employee is left to find their own way in creating a customer experience, inconsistent delivery is the result. Unintentionally, customers receive varying levels of service across touchpoints from initial engagement through sale, product (service) usage, and ongoing support.

Common factors that contribute to inconsistent customer experience include:

- No clear answer to the question: What does a customer get when they choose our offering?
- Lack of standardized processes – e.g., customer engagement approach, sales process, product (service) delivery, ongoing support, proactive customer outreach.
- Communication gaps – Inconsistent, ineffective, or insufficient communications, lack of proactive customer outreach, slow response times to customer inquiries.
- Failure to understand customer preferences – Assuming one size (or communication style) fits all customers overlooks individual differences in information preferences, learning styles, and interests.
- Inadequate employee training and development – Training on the firm's customer experience model (like with the Forklore Restaurant Group), and all aspects of guiding the customer journey is a necessary foundation for delivering a consistent experience.

Recommended Action: Document today's customer journey, then compare the experience with your company's vision. When you identify gaps, use learnings to develop and implement a future state customer journey map.

Unclear or Missing Value Proposition, Failure to Articulate "Why me, why us."

One of the most common questions on the minds of prospective customers is, "Why should I do business with you and your company?" Failure to articulate "why me, why our firm" leaves it up to the prospect to define your value proposition, contributing to a business model issue. Companies and customer-facing employees who cannot answer these questions clearly, succinctly, and deliver on their value proposition are likely to underperform.

Research tells us that the decision process for selecting a service business provider (accountant, attorney, banker, consultant, medical professional) is multifaceted and includes who the customer-facing individual is (background, experience, similar clients), reputation of the firm, trustworthiness of the individual and firm, nature of the offering, value, and perceptions of the individual service provider's ability to consistently deliver.

We also know that relevance as a product or service provider – meaningfulness, pertinence, and importance – must continually be re-earned. Doing a great job yesterday only matters until a new day begins. Therefore, having and communicating a clear value proposition helps contextualize a company's relevance to a customer.

Recommended Action: With clarity about your business's target customer, a company can articulate its value proposition. To achieve the greatest benefit, the value proposition must be well understood, co-owned, and applied by all employees. This will require training, coaching, and ongoing oversight by management.

Activities and Process Design

In a perfect world, activities within an organization are synchronized into processes which align with a clearly defined vision. In reality, many companies perform organizational activities independent of a specific purpose (like fulfilling the company's vision) or are misaligned with success metrics. More activities that do not align with vision fulfillment means resources (human and all other categories) are distracted from advancing the organization.

Activities are building blocks for processes which support other processes across an organization. While precision functions – product assembly, manufacturing, surgery, piloting an airplane – require a well-documented, consistently repeatable series of steps, many business processes are not formalized. However, lack of formal documentation in no way negates the existence of a process. These informal processes can be observed, defined, re-engineered, or discontinued.

Drawbacks to informal processes are inconsistency in performance of activities, overload of information required to properly perform activities, challenges identifying root cause of issues, efficiency limitations, and business model breakdowns.

Banking is a heavily regulated industry and satisfying regulatory requirements is non-negotiable. Yet a common misperception - *policies and procedures are the same thing* - produces unnecessary inefficiencies in the way traditional banks serve customers. How does this happen? Banking regulations emanate from legislation or through a regulatory agency proclamation, the Office of the Comptroller of the Currency for example. New regulations are disseminated to banks for interpretation through their compliance department. Bank compliance departments then distill each regulation into a policy to be followed by bank employees.

Bank regulations impact consumers directly or indirectly, yet it is rare for a bank to define, design and deliver a customer-based process for policy (therefore, regulation) implementation. Banks often lose sight of the intent of a regulation, and by default apply the rule as a process itself. Paradoxically, it is rare for a regulation to *define* a process. Banking regulators generally describe an expected outcome with a new regulation but leave process design to each bank. In this flexibility resides an opportunity for banks to design interoperable processes which satisfy regulators and address existing and emerging customer needs, thereby strengthening their business operating model.

By intentionally framing activities in a process context, leaders reduce risks resulting from individual differences in selecting activities to perform, decrease the likelihood of employees overlooking necessary steps for successful task completion, and create a structure for business model success.

Recommended Action: Vision distils into priorities, strategies, and activities. Work toward synchronizing organizational activities into processes which align with a clearly defined vision. Assess each strategy for alignment with the vision.

Resources

Each business operating model is a recipe for how companies go to market. The necessary resources are required ingredients to operate the business, including human, intellectual and financial capital, technology, physical assets, partnerships, and vendors.

Issues arise when resources misalign with a company's intentionally defined business model. An early-stage fintech firm deployed a go-to-market model built around an app-based financial planning tool. The company promoted the availability of financial planning professionals to answer questions for the do-it-yourself customers who needed some assistance (a majority of their customer base). However, they didn't invest in sufficient staffing for the customer support service. The outcome was negative online reviews and feedback from frustrated users, which damaged the brand. They eventually expanded support service resources, but rebuilding the company's reputation took years.

Recommended Action: Evaluate your company's resource allocation with its vision. The annual budget is a good proxy for asset allocation. How do budgeted expenses align with the vision? Where do adjustments need to be made for optimal alignment?

Economic Model

Your economic model describes costs and scale associated with operating the business relative to the business model and revenue opportunities, and informs marketplace positioning (i.e. low-cost leader, premium offering) and pricing strategy.

Go to Market Model Management

When a business model is at odds with a company's economics, profit margins are an early indicator of issues.

A small, independent pharmacy opened across the street from a large hospital and medical center in the city where I live. It was started by a pharmacist who promoted competitive prices, large inventory, fast prescription preparation time, and friendly service. As an independent, the pharmacist didn't have the scale, purchasing power or technology of her competitors, making it difficult for the business model to succeed.

CVS, with 25% share of the market nationally, was located at the intersection. Walmart (4% share), Ralphs/Kroger (3% share), Albertsons (1% share), and Costco (.6% share) were all located within three miles of this pharmacy. Her economic model was incongruent with the business model, causing the pharmacy to fail in less than six months.

For most types of business, a low-priced provider business model requires high volume, economies of scale, and large scope. Lower volume operations are more likely to succeed though a model built upon differentiation.

Recommended Action: Assess your company's economic model in the context of your target customer, scope, and scale of production. Identify and address gaps between the business and economic models.

Talent Approach

Even in the AI era, it is understood that people are essential to the organization. And it's common for companies to include the importance of their team members in their stated values. The business model breakdown occurs when a disconnect between the stated (or expected) and experienced approach to talent management occurs. When a company's business model calls for highly trained customer service professionals, then fails to provide ongoing staff training, the model is at risk.

Sweetwater is an online musical equipment retailer headquartered in Fort Wayne, Indiana. Founded in 1979, Sweetwater's business model calls for offering "quality instruments and music equipment, expert service, and amazing support"…everything music makers need and more.

Sweetwater customer service representatives are called sales engineers. The company's website says, "These industry insiders don't just sell music gear; they also work with you to come up with smart solutions to your unique challenges. Whether you need an amp rig for your next transatlantic tour or a simple recording setup that fits your budget, you can count on these highly qualified experts." Sounds great, but how does the company support this business model?

I spoke with Jon, a seven-year Sweetwater sales engineer. He explained that as a new employee, all Sweetwater sales engineers receive detailed product training through Sweetwater University (an in-house learning and development resource) across the complete product catalog before engaging directly with customers. Once a sales engineer is on the line, they receive regular new product briefings and ongoing product and technical training. In addition, sales engineers get regular performance feedback from their manager.

Sweetwater sales engineers must have a specialization – guitars, basses, keyboards, mixing, recording and sound equipment, and in most cases, are music makers themselves. Jon is a guitar specialist and plays the instrument. As a guitarist myself, I asked Jon several general and specific guitar questions, and he had answers.

Next, I asked Jon about guitar pedals – sound effects and tone enhancements used by electric guitar players.

Jon said, "I can talk with you about effect pedals, but I have a teammate who specializes in that area. Can I have him join the call to get into details of what you're looking for?"

After speaking with Jon and his colleague, they sent me a YouTube link to a video by Don. Don is a professional guitarist who provides product demos, reviews, how-to's, and group instruction for Sweetwater customers. Sweetwater is an exemplary example of a company that aligns its talent approach with its business model.

Recommended Action: Assess your company's business model requirements of its employees. Ask: how do we know employees are properly prepared for their continually evolving roles? Are team members continually developed, effectively coached, properly managed, and thoroughly engaged? Then develop and implement steps to address all gaps.

Fragmentation

It depends. This chapter began with the pizza franchisee case. Three different pizza experiences based on how a customer's order is placed - one approach to fulfill online orders, a second for phone orders, and a third process for walk-in orders. This is business model fragmentation.

There are times companies appear to think, "It's all about us." Employees operate independently, with different objectives, goals, incentives, and customer experience definitions. What's wrong with this picture? Losing sight of what should matter most: the customer. The root cause is lack of clarity about who the company serves and how they serve them.

In contrast, when a firm's go-to-market operating model starts with the customer, and a clearly defined customer experience roadmap, the dynamic changes. When each person involved in creating the customer experience knows the definition of success, and their individual role in its creation, the company delivers a much stronger performance. A fragmented approach to understanding and addressing customer needs reflects a self-centeredness of the firm vs. what customers deem important.

Recommended Action: De-fragmentation requires an intentionally designed go-to-market business model built around the customer. Review how your company delivers on its offering with an eye for signs of fragmentation or inconsistency. From there, develop and implement a plan to ensure consistent delivery of the desired customer experience.

Chapter 5
Effective Entrepreneurial Leadership

Last spring, I attended the grand opening and ribbon cutting for a new dental practice, a family business operated by the dentist and his wife. With the help of the city's Chamber of Commerce, they orchestrated a wonderful celebration to let the community know the new dental practice was open for business.

The dental office was beautifully appointed, with all new equipment, furnishings, artwork, and decorations. It was clear the business owners had invested heavily in building out the facility and creating a welcoming environment for patients.

I asked the dentist about his journey from making the decision to start his own practice to the grand opening. He explained it had taken about 15 months from the time he and his wife identified the office space, through lease negotiations, interior designs, hiring and coordinating the construction firm to build out the site, working through the city's permitting process, setting up his LLC legal entity structure, buying equipment and furnishings, setting up operating technology (computer systems, telecom, QuickBooks for billing, merchant services card readers), researching and purchasing insurance, establishing bank accounts, developing insurance company relationships for patients' dental insurance reimbursement, and more.

He sounded overwhelmed as he walked through the long list of activities he traversed over the previous year-and-a-quarter to be open for business. I asked about his training in business before, during, or after dental school. He said "I really don't know anything about business. In dental school, I was trained as an oral health doctor. I worked for another dental practice for eight years before deciding to start my own. I had no idea that I would spend over a year managing contractors, dealing with tons of administrative things like getting set up with insurance companies to get paid for the care I provide, or dealing with all the technology stuff we need to make the practice work. And now that we're officially open, I realize only a few of the patients I cared for at the previous practice are following me to my own practice. That means I must spend a lot of time everyday marketing and promoting my practice, figuring out how to compete with other dentists in the area, and finding ways to build the practice so I can do what I was trained to do – care for my patients!"

The conversation with the dentist-turned entrepreneur was enlightening. He was clear about his greatest strength in business – delivering dental care. He was also developing his understanding of all other activities required to build a successful dental practice. As an entrepreneur, he now must work *on* his business as well as working *in* his business (more on this theme in the next chapter). At this point in the journey, the dentist was presented with the opportunity to learn about Effective Entrepreneurial Leadership.

Effective Entrepreneurial Leadership is the capacity of an entrepreneur to drive a venture forward by aligning vision with execution through deliberate, focused action. It is characterized by the ability to establish clear priorities that guide decision-making and resource allocation, ensuring that time and energy are invested where they create the most value. Effective entrepreneurial leaders manage time with discipline and intention, recognizing it as one of their most limited and valuable assets.

Individual strengths and deliberate focused action stand out in this definition of entrepreneurial leadership. Central to this form of leadership is a deep understanding of one's personal strengths, how to optimize them, and a commitment to building upon them, leveraging your unique capabilities. Equally important is the ability to balance efficiency (doing things right) with effectiveness (doing the right things) so that operational excellence supports strategic progress. Through this dual focus, effective entrepreneurial leadership becomes a blend of purpose-driven strategy and practical execution, enabling entrepreneurs to navigate uncertainty, seize opportunity, and build ventures that endure.

We discussed alignment of vision with execution in Chapter 3. This chapter explores combining personal strengths with creating capacity for deliberate, focused action.

Personal Strengths

It has been said that we are all incompetent at many things. The crucial question is not how to turn incompetence into excellence, but to ask, *what can I do uncommonly well?*

Management thought leader Peter Drucker believed our first responsibility is to determine our own distinctive competences - what we can do uncommonly well, then navigate life and career in direct alignment. To focus on fixing weakness is not only foolish; it is irresponsible. To achieve the greatest results, one must use all the available strengths, making them fully productive.

Knowing what one does uncommonly well is an essential ingredient in a successful entrepreneurial enterprise. Perhaps your greatest strength is ideation, process design, or trend analysis to infer new needs within a market.

In the case of the dentist in the story at the beginning of this chapter, I suspect his greatest strength is contextualizing the connection between oral health and overall physical wellbeing.

Although you know your strengths innately, it can be valuable to think through these questions:

What are my top 2-3 strengths?

How can I build upon these strengths?

How can I spend more time in my strength zone in my business?

What is the connection between using my strengths and success in my business?

One powerful resource in understanding and leveraging individual strengths is the Gallup CliftonStrengths (previously known as StrengthsFinder). Based on Don Clifton's research at the University of Nebraska beginning in 1950, Gallup CliftonStrengths has grown to a globally recognized tool used in business, academia, and government to guide people in understanding individual strengths. This tool helps discover what we naturally do best, learn how to develop our greatest talents into strengths, and how to maximize our potential.

CliftonStrengths categorizes the 34 most common human strengths into four aggregate domains: Executing, Influencing, Relationship Building, and Strategic Thinking. After completing a brief assessment, participants learn their top 5 strengths, and how best to apply and develop them.

Whether you use Gallup Clifton Strengths, another self-assessment resource, or simply perform your on self-inventory, a clear focus on your strengths contributes to you entrepreneur's journey by:

- Reinforcing what you do uncommonly well.
- Helping understand what is outside your strength zone.
- Highlighting areas/activities to consider outsourcing or hiring people with the strengths needed to help your business succeed.
- Avoid wasting time doing things you don't do well.

Deliberate, Focused Action: Owning your calendar and time blocking

One of my favorite Peter Drucker books is *The Effective Executive*. Though written in 1966, the lessons remain as applicable today as when the book was first published. The overriding message is that we can learn effectiveness – *doing the right things* (Drucker contrasts effectiveness with efficiency, which he defines as *doing things right*). A foundational step to enhance one's effectiveness is to *know thy time.*

Per Drucker, effective executives (and for our purposes, entrepreneurs) don't start with their tasks, they start with their time. They don't start with a personal plan, they start by finding out *where their time goes*, then attempt to manage their time to make the greatest possible impact through their work.

Everyone has the same number of hours available every day, yet some people are extraordinarily effective in how and where they invest their time, while others, in Drucker's words, are *strikingly ineffectual*.

It is exciting to start or scale a new business. Bringing new ideas to life, a clear business plan, new goals, and aspirations personally, and for your business. Yet, how and where entrepreneurs focus and invest their time is an essential element in business plan execution effectiveness. There are always competing priorities, which means the ability to filter out distractions is a highly coveted skill. Let's deconstruct how you can make the most of your time to advance the business.

Adjusted for holidays and weekends, there are about 248 business days each year, 62 days per quarter, and roughly 21 operating days per month (note: this assumes a 5-day business week; these numbers for retail or B2C businesses is higher; it goes without saying, entrepreneurs work far beyond "regular" business hours, however, similar time allocation ratios still hold true; these numbers are illustrative). Most entrepreneurs estimate that 70%-80% of their time is not allocated at their discretion, meaning time is consumed by necessary administrative tasks, managing technology to operate the firm, time required by other stakeholders like investors, bankers, accountants, attorneys, licensing agencies, regulators, auditors, and the like). This distills into 13 days per quarter (in aggregate), roughly 130 hours of discretionary time, meaning the time you *control* on your calendar, to amplify your impact.

The entrepreneurial leadership question: How will you invest those hours to make your most meaningful impact to advance your business? How will you select the most impactful activities, performed effectively, each available hour this month to move your business as far as possible in the direction toward your long-term vision?

Effective Entrepreneurial Leadership

Entrepreneurial effectiveness stems from consciously consolidating blocks of discretionary time available during the week, then allocating one block of time for intentional, meaningful activities. For example, when you isolate 60 minutes a day for a specific purpose, you can combine the time into a 5-hour block dedicated to valuable tasks like product development, focused marketing, social media management, networking, or proactive relationship management.

In my coaching work and in managing my own time, I use a set of practices that make a significant difference in effectiveness:

- **Own your discretionary time.** Every entrepreneur engages in nondiscretionary activities only peripherally related to our business. Most people control the remainder of their daily calendar time at work. Owning your discretionary time means distinguishing between nondiscretionary activities and those you choose to invest in.
- **Categorize how you invest your time.** Apply simple activity categorization to your calendar to draw your attention to areas you can improve. Make the categories relevant to you, but simple, like *Administrative Tasks*, *Relationship Time*, *New Ventures* (new products, projects, and ideas, business development, new clients), *Talent Time* (developing people on your team, coaching or being coached), and *Lost Time* (time you cannot account for when reviewing your calendar).
- **De-emphasize the annual calendar.** It may seem counterintuitive, yet managing exclusively to the annual business plan has drawbacks. Big goals can be

overwhelming. Deconstructing each into digestible pieces that play to your team's competencies makes goals more manageable and better informs the activities necessary for successful fulfillment.

While a company's vision changes infrequently, the path to its fulfillment can change as conditions shift. Managing monthly goals enables greater flexibility when early signs of changing conditions emerge. The best strategic plan is one that guides daily discretionary activities executed in alignment with the long-term vision.

- **Compare plans with activity capacity.** Deconstructing annual and strategic plans into daily activities, performed in increments of 21 business days, enables entrepreneurs to ask: How does the plan compare with our capacity to perform required activities? Can we realistically perform this set of tasks effectively over the next calendar month?

Understanding capacity is a powerful foundation for establishing goals, even those requiring a stretch. "Good to Great" author Jim Collins describes "Big Hairy Audacious Goals" as a powerful mechanism to stimulate progress, as they require building for the long term and exuding a relentless sense of urgency today. Entrepreneurs must combine the drive to achieve aspirational goals with a clear understanding of the company's capacity. From there, they must allocate capacity for the highest, greatest application of all resources.

- **Daily gut checks.** Perhaps the greatest challenge entrepreneurs face is managing their attention.

Effective Entrepreneurial Leadership

Continuous distractions operate like an undercurrent pulling us from our focus. Much of our time is not within our control. Entrepreneurial effectiveness is heavily impacted by the use of discretionary time. Apply attention during discretionary time to those activities where you can have the greatest impact and contribute the largest ROI. Gut check questions are:
- Where will I add the greatest value to the business today?
- How do I make the most of my discretionary time today in alignment with the company's goals?
- Which activities will have the lowest ROI from investing my attention, and should be avoided?

Entrepreneurial leaders set the tone through focus and alignment with business priorities. Making our time count enhances productivity and demonstrates entrepreneurial leadership on a daily basis. You will make the greatest difference today by investing your discretionary time mindfully to have a meaningful impact on advancing your business.

General Comments on Leadership

My book, *Leading from Where you Are* provides more thoughts about what it means to be a leader. Rather than repeat those thoughts here, I simply offer this summary for entrepreneurial leaders:

Leadership is not
- A job title
- Automatic because you started the company

- Having all the answers
- Control
- Getting credit for accomplishments or successes

Leadership is
- The way we show-up in choices and actions
- Influence and impact through ideas, vision, and priorities
- Being attuned to the business environment's perpetual motion and inferring what it means to the company
- A continually evolving learning process vs. a destination

Chapter 6
Working ON Your Business

As an entrepreneur, you work hard. Long days, full calendar, endless to-do lists, customers to serve, employees to manage, problems to solve, fires to put out. At the end of the day, you've used all the gas in your tank, yet it often feels like the business is running you rather than the other way around. Shortcomings as an entrepreneur are not usually due to a lack of effort. A more common root cause is misallocation of activities, symptoms of working *in* your business.

Working **in** your business means doing the work that keeps the lights on today. It's delivering your product or service, engaging with customers, managing staff, closing deals, addressing operational issues, administrative activities, and making sure nothing breaks. These activities are necessary. Without them, there is no business. But there is more.

Working **on** your business is different. It is the work that improves how the business performs tomorrow. It's stepping back to refine your value proposition, redesign processes to scale, clarify your positioning, invest time in marketing strategies that generate demand, build relationships that open new doors, analyze customer feedback, and challenge assumptions about what's really driving (or constraining) growth.

Both types of work (working in and on your business) matter. The challenge is that one frequently crowds out the other. Entrepreneurs naturally gravitate toward working in their business because it feels productive, familiar, and urgent to perform tasks where you have competence and confidence. You get quick feedback. You can check things off the list. You feel needed. For most entrepreneurs, working in the business is the way you got started and began to create results. Ironically, working in the business is often a growth limiting factor, contributing to plateaus.

Working on the business, by contrast, often feels uncomfortable. The payoff is delayed, and outcomes are less certain. It requires reflection, experimentation, and sometimes confronting inconvenient truths about what isn't working. There are fewer external deadlines forcing it, and no customer is calling to demand that you rethink your operating model or reposition your brand.

Entrepreneurs often hear the advice *slow down to speed up*, yet applying it requires discipline, especially when daily operational demands feel urgent. Working **in** the business delivers immediate feedback, visible progress, and a sense of control, while working **on** the business can feel abstract, slower, and less predictable. Working on your business involves reflection, experimentation, and occasionally confronting uncomfortable realities about what is not working. However, this deliberate focus is precisely what enables business acceleration through clearer priorities, stronger infrastructure, better delegation, and more scalable decision-making. In practice, slowing down is not lost time; it is strategic investment that converts reactive effort into purposeful momentum.

Understanding that the behaviors which helped you start the business can become the ones that prevent it from scaling requires candid self-reflection. What once made you indispensable can eventually make you a bottleneck. When all of

Working on Your Business

your time is spent in execution, there is little room for perspective. When there is no perspective, blind spots grow. Processes calcify. Customer expectations shift unnoticed. Competitors evolve while you're busy just getting through the day.

Time invested working on your business tends to generate disproportionate returns. A few hours spent clarifying your ideal customer can eliminate months of wasted sales effort. Streamlining a core process can free up capacity across the entire organization. Strengthening your message can improve every marketing and sales interaction. Building the right relationships can unlock opportunities that brute-force effort never will.

Yet this work is often shortchanged precisely because it doesn't scream for attention.

Whether you are launching a startup, scaling a growing company, or feeling stuck at a frustrating plateau, the ability to work on your business, not just in it, is a definitive entrepreneurial skill.

Practical Steps to Spend More Time Working ON Your Business

Recognizing the difference between working in your business and working on it is important. Acting on that recognition is what creates change. Entrepreneurs rarely "find" time for strategic work. They must deliberately create it. The following practices help shift your efforts from reactive execution working in your business to intentional scaling for growth.

- **Schedule Strategic Time as a Non-Negotiable Commitment.** Time blocking was covered in Chapter 5, and bears repeating. If it isn't blocked on your calendar, operational demands will consume it. Block recurring time weekly or monthly specifically for strategic thinking. Treat this time the same way you would a key customer meeting. No interruptions, no operational discussions, no email triage. The purpose is perspective, not productivity theater. Consistency matters more than duration. Even two focused hours weekly can materially improve clarity and decision quality.

- **Audit Where Your Time Actually Goes.** Most entrepreneurs underestimate how much time is spent on low-leverage activity. Conduct a simple two-week audit to identify:
  - Tasks only you can do
  - Tasks someone else could do with training
  - Tasks that shouldn't be done at all

This exercise reveals delegation gaps which can be a substantive constraint on strategic focus.

- **Build Delegation Infrastructure, Not Just Delegation Events.** Delegation isn't asking someone to "handle this." It requires:
  - Documented processes
  - Clear decision boundaries
  - Performance expectations
  - Feedback loops

When processes replace heroics, entrepreneurs expand cognitive bandwidth for growth focused work.

- **Institutionalize Reflection Cycles.** Growth requires regular pauses. Establish monthly or quarterly reviews focused on:
    - What's working better than expected
    - What's stagnating or declining
    - Emerging risks and opportunities
    - Competitive positioning shifts

Without structured, disciplined reflection, entrepreneurs default to incrementalism rather than meaningful evolution.

- **Strengthen Market Intelligence Habits.** Entrepreneurs frequently become internally focused as their businesses grow. This can be countered by intentionally seeking external performance signals:
    - Customer feedback beyond complaints
    - Industry trend monitoring
    - Competitor positioning analysis
    - Technology or regulatory shifts

Regularly capturing these perspectives prevents strategic drift.

- **Invest in Relationship Capital.** Operational work produces revenue today. Relationships produce opportunities for tomorrow. Allocate intentional time to:
    - Networking within and outside your immediate professional circles
    - Engaging industry peers

- Building relationships with strategic partners, advisors, mentors, community and ecosystem leaders

The importance of networking cannot be overstated as part of building relationship capital. Many pivotal business breakthroughs originate through informal conversations.

Here's the reality: no matter how brilliant, innovative, or creative we are, *relationships* are what grow our business.

That's where professional networking comes in. And if the word "networking" makes you groan, you're not alone. This is the time to rethink it, because professional networking is simply the business of staying connected to people, learning about them, and helping them succeed while opening doors for your own growth.

A friend of mine was a successful attorney with a firm in Newport Beach, California. He started out as an associate, and after a few years with the firm, rather than pursuing the partner track, he decided he wanted to venture out on his own. He set up his corporation, found an office, arranged to share a legal assistant with another solo practitioner, and he was all set to go. Then reality set in: He didn't have any clients.

The firm he left served mid-sized companies in Orange County, and my friend planned on working with the same type of clients. He just didn't have any clients yet. He made an assumption many of us make. It's the "build it and they will come" assumption. Open the law firm, the game development company, MedTech device company, accounting firm, the boba shop, and customers will automatically come to you. Carry that into the digital world, and the assumption says: build the website or LinkedIn page, TikTok account and customers will come to me.

In reality no matter how brilliant we are, what an amazing tech developer, attorney, or plumber we may be, or what an incredible social media presence we have, it's building and managing a network that leads to business growth. Yes, there can be exceptions, but they are just that: exceptions.

What Is Professional Networking?

At its core, professional networking is the art of developing and nurturing relationships. It's not about collecting business cards or maximizing your follower count, it's about making real connections with people you respect, can learn from, and potentially collaborate with. This can mean attending industry events, one-to-one coffee meetings, Zoom visits, as well as other forms of interacting. Developing and maintaining these professional relationships is so meaningful, I've heard it said that one's network is their net worth.

Start Small

Networking doesn't have to feel fake or overwhelming. If you're new to it, start small. Reach out to one person a week, someone you admire, someone you've worked with before, or someone whose work you appreciate. Send a thoughtful message. Ask a genuine questions and practice the Art of Inquiry. Focus on being human, not "selling" yourself.

It's About Quality, Not Quantity

Don't chase after hundreds of connections. Ask yourself: Who do I really want to learn from? Who's already serving the audience I care about? Who's two steps ahead of me in my industry? Focus on connecting with people whose values and goals align with yours. That's where real traction happens.

Give Before You Ask

One of the best ways to become an exceptional networker? Offer value before asking for anything in return. That could be an article you think they'd enjoy, an intro to someone useful, or simply a kind word about their work. Giving first creates trust—and trust is the currency of relationship capital.

Nurture, Don't Neglect

Networking is not a one-and-done event, it's an ongoing process. Think of your network like a garden. You've got to water it. Stay in touch. Check in periodically, even if there's no agenda. Celebrate others' wins. Send updates about your own journey. Offer encouragement. These small touchpoints create strong, long-lasting relationships.

The Follow-Up Is Where the Magic Happens

Meeting someone is only the beginning. If you want that connection to turn into something meaningful, your follow-up matters. Keep it short, specific, and warm. Remind them how you met, mention something you discussed, and suggest a next step if relevant—like a quick call or a resource you promised.

Working on Your Business

Work Smarter, Not Harder

You don't need to attend every networking event in town. Instead, be intentional. Look for groups or communities that are tightly aligned with your goals—professional associations, mastermind groups, alumni communities, or even niche online forums. Choose the spaces where your ideal clients or collaborators already hang out. Then show up consistently.

Know Your Value Proposition

When you meet someone new, and they ask, "So, what do you do?", your answer matters. Not because it must be flashy, but because it should be clear. Your personal value proposition is your answer to the question: "Why you?" Why should someone hire you, partner with you, or refer you? When you know what makes you valuable, others can see it too.

Common Mistakes to Avoid

Many people go into networking trying to "get" something - clients, deals, investors - without offering anything in return, most importantly, development of a relationship. Others treat it as transactional rather than relational. The worst mistake? Ghosting people after the first meeting. If you want your network to work for you, you must work on your network genuinely, consistently, and generously.

Working *on* your business means building more than your service offering or systems. It means building your brand, your reach, and your relationships. Networking isn't a nice-to-have; it's a core business strategy. The good news: it is a skill that gets better the more you practice it.

- **Simplify Before You Scale.** Albert Einstein said "the definition of genius is taking the complex and making it simple" Complexity masquerades as sophistication but often signals process entropy. Regularly ask:
  - Can this process be streamlined?
  - Can decisions move closer to the customer or front line?
  - Are we adding steps that customers don't value?

Scalable businesses are typically simpler, not more complicated.

- **Clarify Your Role as the Business Evolves.** The entrepreneurial skill set that launches a venture is not always the one that scales it. Periodically reassess:
  - Where you add the most value today, compared to when you launched the company
  - Where you may unintentionally be a bottleneck
  - What leadership capabilities the next phase of growth requires

Role evolution is a hallmark of sustainable growth.

- **Measure Strategic Progress, Not Just Operational Output.** Most dashboards track revenue, expenses, and operational KPIs. Add metrics tied to working on the business:
  - New partnerships formed
  - Process improvements implemented
  - Social media reach and impact

Working on Your Business

- o Customer segment penetration
- o Brand awareness or positioning gains

What gets measured tends to receive attention.

The Compounding Effect

Working on your business rarely produces immediate gratification. Its impact is cumulative. Small strategic improvements compound into stronger positioning, clearer execution, and more predictable growth.

Entrepreneurs who master this balance don't necessarily work fewer hours. They work differently. Their effort shifts from constant firefighting to building systems that reduce fires altogether.

This shift from spending more time working on your business is analogous to the transition from bricklayer to architect. It is one of the defining transitions in the entrepreneurial journey.

Working on your business processes

My dad had a friend named Ralph Berol in the business of manufacturing pens. His factory was in Los Angeles, where my family lived. At the time, Ralph's factory was not automated; all pen production was done by hand. When Ralph received large orders requiring quick fulfilment, he needed additional labor for pen assembly to meet customer expectations. To expand production capacity, Ralph asked friends to lend a hand and assemble pens in their homes. He paid one cent per completed pen. To earn extra money for our family, my dad often accepted Ralph's requests. Dad, mom, my brother, and I turned our kitchen table into a makeshift pen production operation.

The Entrepreneur's Journey

My brother and I were in elementary school at the time and the opportunity to earn a penny for every pen we assembled was compelling. One hundred pens per kid meant earning more than our weekly allowance. Ralph delivered boxes containing pen components – an inner spring-loaded ink filler, a push-button click mechanism to engage the filler, the two-piece outer pen body and a silver or gold ornamental ring for installation between the top and bottom pen body pieces.

Our first pen assembly engagements were individual endeavors. Dad placed boxes of components on the kitchen table, we all took our seats, grabbed the pieces we needed, then assembled pens until fatigue set in or we completed the batch.

After completing our first few batches, mom introduced the idea of developing an assembly line process by breaking down pen construction into subassemblies. First step - install a filler into the bottom component of the pen body. Second, insert the push-button click mechanism into the upper body. Third, add the ornamental ring to the bottom pen body. Final step, screw the upper and lower pen body components together and place the completed pen into a box.

This process resulted in accelerating our family pen production work and increasing output capacity. Through this assembly line process, we hit our stride and produced 2,500 pens in a weekend. The lesson: Processes must be defined, designed, and deployed with their goal in mind.

Clearly defined processes enhance effectiveness, efficiency, and consistency across activities. In the book, *Leading from Zero*, I describe the three principles of the "Process Mindset": activity-process connectivity is stronger when intentionally designed, every activity is part of a larger process, and every process must align with a purpose.

Activity-process Connectivity

Activities are building blocks for processes which support other processes across a business. Process is a series of activities or steps taken to fulfill a purpose or achieve an objective. While precision functions – product assembly, manufacturing, surgery, piloting an airplane – require a well-documented, consistently repeatable series of steps, many entrepreneurial business processes are not formalized. However, lack of formal documentation in no way negates existence of a process. These informal processes can be observed, defined, re-engineered, or discontinued.

Drawbacks to informal processes are inconsistency in performance of activities, overload of information required to properly perform activities, challenges identifying root cause of issues, and efficiency limitations. Imagine an emergency room team approaching an incoming patient in crisis without having a clear process for assessing the problem before beginning surgery. Scary, but that's exactly what happened at a hospital in San Francisco.

In *The Checklist Manifesto: How to Get Things Right*, Atul Gawande, a public health researcher and surgeon, described the scenario. The medical team began surgery on a man believed to have suffered a shallow stab wound. Unfortunately, after surgery began, surgeons noticed a much larger, foot-long wound, resulting from being impaled with a bayonet. The man's injury occurred at a Halloween costume party. The surgical team on duty failed to double-check with the patient to understand what kind of injury he experienced.

Dr. Gawande used this example and other case studies to espouse use of a simple process guide known as the checklist. In his words, "The volume and complexity of what we know has exceeded our individual ability to deliver its benefits correctly, safely, or reliably. Knowledge has both saved us and burdened us." Dr. Gawande's research points to improved safety, consistency, and efficiency resulting from use of simple, short checklists. "What is needed…isn't just people working together be nice to each other. It is discipline. We are by nature inconstant creatures. We are not built for discipline. We are built for novelty and excitement, not for careful attention to detail. Discipline is something we must work at. Just ticking boxes is not the goal here. Embracing a culture of teamwork and discipline is."

The challenge of consistency and discipline is not exclusive to the medical field. These principles apply to entrepreneurial activities as well. A checklist is simply an aid – an easy-to-use method of documenting a process. Dr. Gawande's advice for using checklists applies to seeing activities as elements of a process:

- **Keep the Checklist Simple and Short:** When every detail of every step is laid out, it makes the checklist too bulky. It also turns into micromanagement. It is a guideline, not an instruction manual.
- **Use Different Types of Checks for Different Needs:** Critical tasks need different checks than complex tasks. Task checks, such as setting up regular testing for software code, should be applied to critical aspects of a project. These are the aspects that could easily slip a team member's mind but could make a big difference if forgotten about. For more complex areas of a project, it can

be a good idea to set up communication checks. This means that if there's an area of a project that is expected to have potential setbacks, collaboration is key. It helps to remind people that while they are responsible for a task, they aren't working in isolation.
- **Checklists Can Be Used for Learning and for Reminding:** If there is an expert working on a project, their checklist should only be used to confirm they are completing each step. However, for someone with limited experience, a checklist can be used as a learning tool. This individual should read the checklist first, then use it to guide them through the process.
- **Test and Adjust:** It is rare to get a checklist perfect the first time around. Develop a checklist, put it into action, and observe its success. Evaluate which steps are confusing or redundant. You can fix these as you work your way through the list.

Dr. Gawande's work has been applied in business and medicine with positive results. Researchers found that simply having the doctors and nurses in an intensive care unit create their own process checklists for what they thought should be done each day improved the consistency of care to the point that the average length of patient stay in intensive care dropped by half. Imagine what simple, clear process definition can do in your business!

Practicing the Process Mindset principle requires entrepreneurs to step back from any specific activity, understand its interconnectedness, its interoperability with other direct and indirect activities, then evaluate the most effective, efficient, consistently repeatable approach to performing the task in context of the broader business ecosystem.

Interoperability refers to the first element of the Process Mindset - the *activity-process* connectivity. Connectivity extends beyond a single process and emerges from the interaction of diverse activities. Entrepreneurs are accountable for identifying and understanding relationships and assuring continuous process improvement.

Smart manufacturing developments present *Process Mindset* learnings applicable to overall business activity connectedness. In their study, *Interoperability in Smart Manufacturing: Research Challenges,*[7] researchers Abe Zeid, Sarvesh Sundaram, Mohsen Moghaddam, Sagar Kamarthi and Tucker Marion of the Department of Mechanical and Industrial Engineering, Northeastern University, explored the increasing need for interoperability at different levels of the manufacturing ecosystem in context of recent advances in manufacturing technology - cyber-physical systems, industrial internet, artificial intelligence, and machine learning.

In these researchers' words, smart manufacturing involves networking of heterogenous components and services that reside within the boundaries of a factory (e.g., integration of smart shop-floor devices) or beyond (e.g., integration of a manufacturing cell with a cloud-based service). The integration and networking of smart manufacturing components and services within and beyond the boundaries of the factory call for seamless exchange of information with syntax and semantics understandable by all the heterogeneous systems involved. This

---

[7] https://www.mdpi.com/2075-1702/7/2/21/ht

interconnectivity is interoperability - the ability of two or more entities (or processes) to interact and cooperate. The study's authors believe successful implementation of enterprise-wide interoperability would result in effective and smooth manufacturing operations, cost reductions, increased productivity, and product quality.

As applied to the entrepreneur's journey, interoperability aligns with the first element of the Process Mindset - the *activity-process* connection.

Through the lens of the larger Process

Recognition that activities are part of some larger process, not standalone events, is a first step in evaluating consistency, effectiveness, and efficiency. Consider the example of commercial air travel. An overarching process encompasses a series of activities - subprocesses – to fulfill the purpose of transporting passengers and cargo safely. The flight itself is the larger process. Supporting the flight are light and heavy aircraft maintenance processes, interior and exterior cleaning, preflight checklist procedure and fueling processes. Each individual procedure is part of the larger process. When each process is performed effectively, the outcome is more likely to fulfill the purpose. If a procedure is missed or performed ineffectively, fulfilling the purpose faces increased risk.

In 1982, Boeing introduced the 767, a twin engine, long-range wide-body airplane. The 767 could be configured to carry 269 passengers and cargo 6,500 nautical miles. The plane came equipped with three redundant hydraulic systems for operation of controls, landing gear, and utility systems and a Ram Air Turbine[8] to power basic controls in the event of an emergency

---

[8] https://en.wikipedia.org/wiki/Ram_air_turbine

that compromised power. This feature saved the day in 1983 when an Air Canada 767 ran out of fuel during flight at an altitude of 41,000 feet.

Flight 143 originated in Montreal, with a scheduled stop in Ottawa in route to Edmonton. Pilots and ground support technicians performed their preflight procedures as required. One step involved accessing information provided by the Fuel Quantity Information System Processor (FQIS) which controls fuel pumps and feeds information to the plane's fuel gauges. Due to a sensor malfunction, the FQIS didn't work that day, leaving the 767 without operating fuel gauges. However, redundancies existed to navigate this type of event.

In this situation, plan 'B' called for the flight maintenance crew to calculate fuel in the 767's tanks manually by a process known as "dipping the tanks" - the jet plane version of using an oil dipstick in a car - to determine onboard fuel volume. Fuel technicians cautiously worked through their calculations to assure sufficient fuel for the scheduled flight.

Employee training is an important subprocess supporting the macro-process of completing safe flights. In this case, the flight maintenance crew had not been trained to perform manual fuel dip calculations. Since technicians were unfamiliar with this process on the new Boeing 767, they re-ran measurements three times for an accurate read. With proper training, they would have known the 767 used all metric measurements; instead, they assumed U.S. measurements in assessing fuel levels. One kilo equals 2.2 pounds, so their measurements overstated fuel on board by about double.

At the first stop in Ottawa, the 767's fuel tanks were re-dipped, and again, the measurements overstated fuel by double.

Working on Your Business

Actual fuel onboard totaled 9,144 kilos at departure from Ottawa. Fuel required to reach Edmonton was about 20,000 kilos.

Over Red Lake, Ontario, a warning light came on in the cockpit informing pilots of a fuel pressure problem with the left engine. Soon, a second fuel pressure warning light illuminated. After evaluating the situation, the pilot prepared for an unscheduled landing in Winnipeg. As the plane descended to an altitude of 28,000 feet, the left engine flamed out. Moments later, starved of fuel, the right engine failed. Miscalculating fuel in the plane's tanks turned this new Boeing 767 into 132-ton glider.

The outcome of this experience could have been tragic, but a series of factors came together to prevent disaster. When both engines failed, the 767's Ram Air Turbine deployed, descended from the plane's undercarriage and activated the wind-driven fan supplying hydraulic pressure necessary to operate certain fight controls. This back-up system bought pilots time to develop a plan to land their aircraft.

In addition to commercial aviation experience, the plane's pilot, captain Robert Pearson, had experience as a glider pilot, a skillset that elevated his ability to navigate this extraordinary situation. However, Winnipeg airport was beyond glide range, and no large airports existed in the area, limiting landing options. Co-pilot Maurice Quintal introduced an alternative to a commercial airport. While in the Royal Canadian Air Force, Quintal had been stationed at a now abandoned base in Gimli. He knew the site's runways were long enough to land the 767 and suspected the base lay within glide range. Quintal and Pearson performed glide speed and descent calculations with support from air traffic control to pinpoint their landing at the Gimli base.

The Entrepreneur's Journey

As the Gimli runways came into line of sight, Pearson noticed a large group of people congregated at the site. The runways had been turned into an auto racetrack. That Saturday afternoon they hosted the Winnipeg Sports Car Club's Family Day event. When people at the track saw the big plane coming in, they scattered as fast as possible to get out of the way.

Through deft aviation skill, captain Pearson overcame lack of drive brakes and engine controls to slow the plane to landing speed. The second the rear wheels hit the ground the captain pumped the brakes. Two tires blew out. The front landing gear had not properly locked into place and collapsed as the front wheels hit the runway, causing the plane's nose to skid on the tarmac. Miraculously, there were no injuries from the landing.[9]

This story provides a dramatic illustration of the Process Mindset applicable to your entrepreneurial endeavors. Training is an important, ongoing process in an organization, not a standalone event. This training process is aligned with a purpose – assuring that all employees are fully enabled to accurately, competently, perform their jobs. The training subprocess supports the larger process of safely transporting passengers and cargo.

Less dramatic, yet aligned with the Process Mindset principle, are activities like new product development, manufacturing, marketing, business development, distribution, and the customer experience, all of which contribute to earning, re-earning, and sustaining relevance as a business.

---

[9] http://hawaii.hawaii.edu/math/Courses/Math100/Chapter1/Extra/CanFlt143.htm

Working on Your Business

Process aligned with Purpose

Process needs purpose. It goes without saying. Or does it? A recent study by OnePoll[10] found that one-third of office-based employees' time is wasted on *pointless* business processes. Fifty-one percent of the survey's 5,000 respondents said outdated business processes were preventing them from doing their jobs properly. The need to assure process relevance, alignment with purpose, extends beyond office workers.

Robotic Process Automation (RPA) is technology that emulates human activities within digital systems to create and automate rules-based business processes. RPA enables process streamlining, efficiency and reduced operating costs. In their *Harvard Business Review* article *Before Automating Your Company's Processes, Find Ways to Improve Them*,[11] authors Thomas H. Davenport[12] and David Brain[13] wrote, "In many companies, the level of process knowledge and understanding is quite low. The company may have collections of standard operating procedures, but they are often poorly documented and out of date. Each employee typically follows their understanding of best practices."

Davenport and Brian are proponents of RPA: "What sets RPA apart from other automation technologies is that its ability to imitate a human user of one or more information systems reduces development time and extends the range of functions that can be automated across a much wider range of business activities."

---

[10] https://www.financialdirector.co.uk/2019/06/19/how-inefficient-processes-waste-nearly-a-third-of-employees-time/
[11] https://hbr.org/2018/06/before-automating-your-companys-processes-find-ways-to-improve-them
[12] https://hbr.org/search?term=thomas%20h.%20davenport
[13] https://hbr.org/search?term=david%20brain

They qualify their views, writing, "To be clear, however, the match between RPA and business processes isn't a perfect one if the goal is to redesign or improve the process rather than to automate its current state, quoting the words of process management expert Andrew Spanyi[14], who said, 'RPA does not redesign anything. It doesn't ask whether we need to do this activity at all. It operates at the task level and not the end-to-end process level.'"

This underscores the importance of defining process purpose in context of earning relevance. Absent clear purpose underlying a process, resources are distracted, misallocated or inefficient, even with use of cutting-edge software like RPA. Establishing the processes purpose results from answering three questions:

- Is this process necessary in executing our business strategy; if so, why?
- What is the expected outcome of the series of activities which comprise this process?
- If we didn't perform this process, how would we achieve the expected outcome?

Process Mindset Applied

Entrepreneurs demonstrating the Process Mindset discern interconnectedness of activities, see activities as part of a larger process aligned with a purpose. By intentionally framing activities in a process context, leaders reduce risks resulting from individual differences in selecting activities to perform, decrease the likelihood of employees overlooking necessary steps for successful task completion, and create a structure for continuous improvement.

---

[14] http://www.spanyi.com

Working on Your Business

Strategy development is deductive, beginning with defining a future state vision. The picture of what things will look like because of intentional business activities is deconstructed into strategies, implemented through activities. Process definition is inductive, aligning activities which support strategy implementation, in a sequence that optimizes efficiency and effectiveness. Process design provides a connecting point between vision and execution to assure activities produce desired outcomes. By integrating top-down with bottom-up approaches, leaders create an environment biased toward activities designed for purpose fulfilment.

Putting the Process Mindset into practice requires five steps:
- Affirm a clear future state vision for your organization.
- Assess each strategy for alignment with the vision.
- Assess each activity supporting a strategy for alignment.
- Evaluate activities for interconnectedness with others' process connectivity.
- Bundle connected activities into processes, designing for efficiency and effectiveness.

Each step requires studied, purposeful diagnostics, candid evaluation, and openness to redesign. The payoff for operating with a disciplined Process Mindset is a more effective, efficient business model, well positioned to earn and re-earn relevance with the company's stakeholders every day.

Working on the way your business is seen
"Mirror mirror on the wall, who's the fairest of them all?" Grimm's fairy tale tells the story of an evil queen in a distant land.

Each time she asked this question of her magic mirror, she heard the same answer: "Thou, O Queen, art the fairest of all." This pleased the queen since she knew her magical mirror spoke nothing but the truth.

One fine morning the queen asked, "Mirror, mirror on the wall, who's the fairest of them all?"

The mirror's answer shocked her. "You, my queen, are fair; it is true. But Snow White is even fairer than you."

The queen reacted with rage. "Huntsman, take Snow White into the woods and kill her. When you come back be sure to bring Snow White's heart as proof she is dead."

The huntsman took Snow White into the forest but found himself unable to kill her. Instead, he let her go and brought the queen the heart of a wild boar as evidence he completed his assignment.

Seeing ourselves as others see us challenges our nature. While self-awareness is unique to the human species, we are generally poor judges of the way others perceive us. Social science research tells us we often overestimate our level of self-awareness. We feel we know and understand ourselves, and how others see us, better than we do. To try to see ourselves objectively can trigger difficult-to-process feelings. Consequently, we avoid, minimize, or rationalize observations we don't like. Our brains are wired for fight or flight, which predisposes us to protect ourselves against negative feedback.

Like the evil queen, our bias is to see ourselves in a favorable light. We emphasize our positives, discount our negatives. This is not just a phenomenon of the social media era. Organizational research supports this. Studies show employees routinely rate themselves above average relative to their peers. A classic study performed six decades ago, *Participation and the Appraisal System,* by John French, Jr.[15], Emanuel Kay,[16] and Herbert H. Meyer[17], researched performance self-assessments at a General Electric plant in 1965.[18]

This study analyzed 92 performance reviews. On average, reviews covered 32 specific performance items with positive appraisals on 19 items and negative on 13. Praise more often related to general performance characteristics, while criticism usually focused on specific performance improvement items.

When receiving feedback, the average employee reacted defensively to seven of their manager's critiques during the appraisal meeting (about 54% of the time). Observers recorded denial of shortcomings cited by the manager, blaming others, and excuses as defensive reactions.

Managers rarely observed constructive responses to critiques. The more negative feedback the employee received during the performance appraisal meeting, the more defensively he reacted (all participants were men in this study). Researchers posit one explanation for defensiveness: the difference between an employee's self-assessment and the manager's appraisal.

The most interesting take-away from this study: On average, employees perceived their performance to be *above* average in their self-assessment. Only two of the 92 participants estimated their performance below average. For the remaining 90 employees, the average self-estimate of performance was at the 77th percentile, which means the average employee saw themselves as 27 points above average, a *statistically impossible*

---

[15] https://journals.sagepub.com/doi/10.1177/001872676601900101
[16] https://journals.sagepub.com/doi/10.1177/001872676601900101
[17] https://journals.sagepub.com/doi/10.1177/001872676601900101
[18] https://hbr.org/1965/01/split-roles-in-performance-appraisal

result! The evil queen's reaction in the story of Snow White was extreme. Feeling shocked by uncomfortable feedback is common.

Clearly, seeing ourselves objectively as individuals is a challenge. Is the dilemma different for our entrepreneurial businesses? Yes and no.

Businesses are complex social networks comprised of individuals, therefore subject to human conditions. Seeing our business as others do is critical to earning, re-earning, and sustaining relevance in the marketplace.

How do businesses overcome the natural tendency toward not being objective?

Globally, companies spend $50 billion annually on market research to understand customers, market trends, competition, and how the market perceives a business and its products. An abundance of available feedback provides leaders rich insights into how others see their organization.

Direct, unvarnished views on how employees and customers see a business, accessible through Glassdoor, Foursquare, Yelp, Angie's List, Slant, and others, enables leaders to put themselves in the shoes of their most valuable stakeholders.

Stakeholder insights and research become valuable when they inform actions that lead to better employee and customer experiences, greater value-add, or identification of blind spots in the way a company shows up.

Yet, even with the petabytes of data companies gather about their customers, preferences, behaviors, and perceptions about relevance are overlooked. Why? Organizational Self-Awareness

Organizational self-awareness means understanding stakeholders' perceptions of how your business shows up. Leadership literature is flush with material on the importance of individual self-awareness. Ingredients for leadership success include the ability to monitor ourselves, attune to our emotions and understand how we come across to others, read our audience, and make adjustments to meet situation-specific needs.

Effective self-awareness shines a light on blind spots, informs actions, sets parameters for reactions, and empowers a feedback loop that reflects the impact of our words and actions. People who demonstrate heightened self-awareness are more effective leaders. Absent self-awareness, people in leadership positions appear tone-deaf, out of touch, ignorant or arrogant.

Organizational self-awareness is a corollary. A company fuels this when it institutionalizes mechanisms to override natural blind spots, including employee and customer feedback assimilation processes, peer listening reviews, issue recognition forgiveness, find it/fix-it empowerment, and new employee observation downloads. These activities help acquire and sustain a clear line-of-sight into the way your company is perceived:

- **Implement employee and customer feedback assimilation processes.** The purpose of each feedback process is to gather stakeholder observations while overriding the tendency toward Situational Attribution - attributing the cause of perceptions (behaviors) to a situation or event outside a person's control rather than an internal characteristic.
- **Practice a well-defined, ongoing method** for acquiring and assimilating perceptions reflective of the company's relevance to its stakeholders. Assimilating employee and customer perspectives are essential ingredients to relevance. Entrepreneurs must recognize they own the company's vision; stakeholder perspectives on relevance

informs them how effectively stakeholders interpret steps to implement the business vision. An effective process for assimilating perceptions from employees or customers about your organization includes:

- **Obtain feedback from employees and customers through multiple comfortable, safe channels.** A single-channel approach (i.e., employee engagement surveys) will miss opportunities with stakeholders uncomfortable in the chosen format. For example, customer focus groups can generate candid feedback. However, participants differ in comfort levels with direct, forthright, in-person sharing. Conversely, online surveys invite anonymous feedback to specific questions. At the same time, this platform allows biases (i.e., answering survey questions the way respondents believe they are expected to answer), and exaggerated feedback (amplifying a complaint or compliment). Using multiple channels to gather diverse input yields actionable feedback.
- **Engage objective, candid feedback trustees,** advisors who act in the organization's best interest when they share unvarnished feedback to inform actions. Advisors can be consultants, customer user groups, advisory board members, community influencers, or other external observers willing to share feedback in the company's best interest.
- **Commit to receive feedback without judgement.** To withhold root cause analysis of a perception until feedback is sufficiently received is difficult and requires discipline to fight urges to defend, rationalize or explain the situation while gathering feedback. For the company

to commit to suspend analysis, judgement, blame, or reaction requires practice, but pays a valuable dividend in the form of deep awareness of the organization's relevance with stakeholders.

- **Peer Listening Reviews.** Each employee in an organization lives a unique experience of its activities that informs individual perspectives. These views can be mined to stretch organizational self-awareness. Peer-to-peer listening can be simple – recurring one-to-one meetings between two employees with an agenda covering observations of the organization overall and areas of responsibility for each person in the meeting. The approach can also be formal, documented and disseminated across the team.
- **Issue Recognition Hold-harmless.** "The first messenger that gave notice of Lucullus'[19] coming was so far from pleasing to Tigranes[20] that he had his head cut off for his pains; and no man dared to bring further information. Without any intelligence at all, Tigranes sat while war was already blazing around him, giving ear only to those who flattered him." Greek philosopher and author Plutarch[21] made it clear in *Lives of the Noble Greeks and Romans* that the bearer of bad news faces existential risks. Conversely, penalizing the messenger does not further organizational self-awareness.

---

[19] https://en.wikipedia.org/wiki/Lucullus
[20] https://en.wikipedia.org/wiki/Tigranes_II
[21] https://en.wikipedia.org/wiki/Plutarch

According to Gallup,[22] when things go horribly wrong for a business, two factors are almost always true: Someone in the company knew about the issue and someone didn't speak up. More than likely, they didn't speak up because they couldn't be bothered, or they feared retaliation. Unfortunately, many entrepreneurs attempt to patch over these systemic problems with policy changes when the underlying issue is cultural.

To embed a hold-harmless commitment into organizational culture enables team members to explore opportunities and see things as do other stakeholders. By removing fear for potential bearers of any news – good, bad, or neutral - the organization multiplies its points of observation and insight. Confident employees rise to expectations for issue recognition, articulation, and resolution.

- **Find It/Fix It Empowerment.** Empowering employees to find and fix issues that interfere with the customer experience is a corollary to the Hold-harmless principle. Gallup says, "A [company] culture that doesn't handle problems well is especially damaging when those problems are connected to customers. Gallup has discovered that customer relationships can be saved *and strengthened* when customers feel heard, businesses genuinely apologize, and something is done to make things right. How to 'make things right' will depend on that customer's unique needs. How that customer feels about the way their issue was handled will significantly affect their opinion of your business and their recommendations to others."

---

[22] https://www.gallup.com/workplace/323165/why-isn-brand-bigger-data-point-one-answer.aspx

Chapter 7
Why You?

A colleague of mine left a management position at an investment firm to start a FinTech company. He saw a need in the marketplace in his time with the investment firm that nobody seemed to be addressing.

He framed his solution, hired developers, built and tested a prototype, refined it, and prepared to launch. He invested three years building an elegant, technically sophisticated product. It worked. It solved the problem. It was smart. Now he needed funding to scale.

He identified venture capital firms that invested in FinTech. He secured pitch meetings. He built a detailed presentation deck that showcased the market landscape, the architecture of his system, the regulatory nuances, the logic behind his product design, and the complexity of the algorithms driving it.

He invited me to join a few of his pitches to offer feedback. Most meetings followed the same pattern. The investors were polite. They asked a few clarifying questions. Then came some version of the same response:

"This is interesting... but we don't really see the upside."

After dozens of pitches, one investor said something refreshingly direct: "Can you simplify your story? I understand you're smart. But you're going way too deep into how this works. I don't care about the intricacies yet. I care about why it matters. What's the problem you are addressing? How are you solving it?

What's the return? Tell me why this is a big opportunity. Don't show me how smart you are."

The investor was right. Unfortunately, my colleague was offended. He took the feedback as an insult to his intelligence. He believed that if people truly understood his expertise, they would appreciate the brilliance of his solution.

Here's the truth: Investors don't fund brilliance. Customers don't buy brilliance. Employees don't join brilliance. They respond to clarity.

The Curse of Knowledge

What my colleague was experiencing is something psychologists call *the curse of knowledge*. Once you know something deeply, it becomes difficult to imagine what it's like not to know it.

Entrepreneurs often fall into this trap. The deeper their expertise, the more they explain. The more they explain, the more complex their story becomes. And the more complex their story becomes, the more confused their audience feels.

Clarity is not a measure of intelligence. Clarity is a measure of discipline. Your audience doesn't need your depth first. They need relevance. You earn the right to go deep only after you make your business story (product or service) matter.

Why Value Proposition Clarity Determines Momentum

Entrepreneurs who can explain their value proposition clearly and concisely dramatically improve their odds of success — with customers, investors, and talent.

When your message is vague:
- Investors question product-market fit.

Why You?

- Customers hesitate.
- Employees struggle to align.
- Marketing becomes expensive.
- Sales cycles stretch.
- Strategy drifts.

When your message is clear:
- Stakeholders quickly understand the opportunity.
- Risk feels manageable.
- The upside feels tangible.
- Decisions accelerate.

Clarity signals strategic maturity. Investors often reject opportunities not because of financials, but because founders cannot articulate what problem they solve, for whom, and why it matters. When founders ramble, it suggests weak positioning, undefined differentiation, or an immature business model. A concise value proposition communicates:
- You know your customer.
- You understand their pain.
- You've identified a meaningful opportunity.
- You have a focused strategy.
- You're capable of disciplined execution.

That is what inspires confidence.

What is a Value Proposition?

Your value proposition answers one question: Why should someone do business with you? It is a clear, concise statement that explains:

- Who you serve
- What problem you solve
- What benefit you deliver
- Why you are different

A powerful value proposition is informed by:
- **Target Customer** – The specific segment you serve.
- **Problem or Need Addressed** – The pain point or opportunity.
- **Unique Benefit** – A meaningful result or outcome of your offering.
- **Differentiation** – Why you, instead of alternatives.

Weak vs. Strong: The Difference

Notice the difference in these contrasting value proposition examples:

- **Weak:** "We've developed a proprietary AI-enabled financial optimization platform leveraging advanced behavioral modeling and algorithmic allocation frameworks."

- **Stronger:** "We help independent investors grow their portfolios with automated strategies that outperform traditional advisors at half the cost."

Why You?
This chapter isn't just about why your business. It's also about why *you*. Investors fund founders. Customers trust credibility.

Why You?

Employees follow conviction. When you articulate why you are the right person to lead this mission, your value proposition becomes credible. It becomes believable.

The First-Impression Reality

First impressions form quickly—often within seconds. And once formed, they are hard to reverse. If stakeholders struggle to understand what you do or why it matters, you may not get a second meeting.

On shows like *Shark Tank*, you see this repeatedly. Founders who ramble lose investor attention within seconds. In real life, it's no different. If you cannot explain your business succinctly, scaling sales becomes difficult. If you can't equip your team with a clear message, marketing becomes inconsistent. If employees don't understand the vision, alignment suffers.

If your value proposition is unclear, every other decision becomes more expensive.

A Simple Framework

If you're new to defining your business value proposition, here is a simple prompt to begin the process:

"We help [target customer] solve [specific problem] by [unique solution]. Unlike alternatives, we [clear differentiator]."

Make it fit your business, then pressure-test it with potential customers, partners, network colleagues, and professional peers. Once you have a sample value proposition, ask yourself if it answers these questions:

- Who specifically do I serve?
- What problem or need do my prospective customers have that I will address?

- What meaningful result will I deliver?
- How is my offering different?
- Why is my business uniquely positioned to succeed?
- If I shared this value proposition with my grandparents, would they understand it?

Your answers may inform you how to refine the value proposition or encourage you to use it in moving full speed ahead. Remember, complex businesses still require simple explanations.

Returning to My Colleague

Eventually, after enough rejection, my colleague did simplify his story. Instead of leading with system architecture and domain expertise, he began leading with the problem his company committed to address. He clearly shared his story, and the need he addressed. He highlighted the upside and reduced technical detail until requested.

The result? Meetings improved. Conversations became more engaged. Investors leaned in instead of leaning back. The product hadn't changed. His value proposition did change.

Final Thought

Entrepreneurs often believe success depends on how innovative their solution is. In reality, success is more driven by how well we tell our story, and why it matters.

Your value proposition is not a slogan. Entrepreneurs who can explain their value proposition clearly and concisely dramatically improve their odds of success with customers, investors, and talent because clarity signals strategic maturity.

Why You?

Investors often reject opportunities not just due to overvaluation or financials, but because founders cannot quickly articulate what problem they solve, for whom, and why it matters. When the message is vague, it raises doubts about product-market fit, scalability, and leadership readiness. Clear articulation, by contrast, suggests disciplined thinking, credible execution capability, and a business model grounded in real demand rather than aspiration.

This clarity also directly impacts market traction and team building. Customers are more likely to buy what you have to offer when they immediately understand the benefit. Investors are more likely to fund when a company's value proposition is well articulated, opportunity is tangible, and risk appears manageable. Prospective employees engage more readily when they can see the company's vision, strategy, and growth potential. A concise value proposition distills strategy into an understandable message, aligning priorities, activities, marketing, investment positioning, and recruiting around a unified narrative. Entrepreneurs who master this practice tend to secure funding more easily, accelerate customer adoption, and attract stronger talent because stakeholders can quickly grasp why the company exists and what success looks like.

When you can answer "Why you?" clearly and confidently, you reduce friction, accelerate trust, and increase opportunity.

And when opportunity increases, your business begins to work for you, rather than the other way around.

Chapter 8
The Entrepreneur as Change Leader

A couple of years ago, my son and I visited the Porsche Driving Experience in Los Angeles. I love cars, especially German sports cars, making this a great father-son outing.

The session included a performance driving coach and 90 minutes behind the wheel of two different Porsche cars – an electric Taycan Turbo and a 640 horsepower 911 Turbo. With in-depth guidance from my coach, I raced a 1.3-mile handling course, designed to emulate a canyon road, with tight corners and long straightaways, an ice hill that simulates slippery mountain conditions, and a kick-plate which causes loss of vehicle control so drivers can learn to navigate unexpected conditions.

As part of the performance driving training, my coach said, "The two things that matter most in driving through expected and unanticipated conditions are vision and alignment. Keep your focus on where you're going, then make sure your steering and pedal control align."

The same principles apply to leading change: Two things that matter most are vision (success: your business defined) and alignment (how the company manifests its vision)!

Change Leadership

For entrepreneurs, Change Leadership refers to proactive ongoing adaptation of an organization to its operating environment, which is in perpetual motion. Change Leadership, as an element of strategic management, is an ongoing, dynamic process. Why? Operating conditions are in perpetual motion. Entrepreneurs must be attuned to conditions in the present moment to infer and inform actions taken today, aligned with their future state success.

Entrepreneurs have a choice: intentionally initiate adaptive organizational change or react to forces which *will* evolve the business. Vision sets the course, then informs actions defined by the business operating model. In the words of my performance driving coach, vision and alignment (with the business model) are the foundation of effective change leadership.

An important distinction is the difference between *change leadership* as an element of every entrepreneur's responsibility and *change management* endeavors. The principle: operating conditions are in perpetual motion, thus navigating change is simply business as usual. In contrast, *change management* projects are events with a beginning, middle, and end. Most often, change management efforts are a reaction to something like changes in customers' expectations, and the competitive, economic, technological, regulatory, or resource environment.

Mark Twain wrote "The only person who likes change is a baby with a wet diaper." Twain may be right. Yet navigating change is essential for effective entrepreneurial leadership. Every entrepreneur has a choice: proactively initiate pre-emptive change or react to change-inducing events.

In change leadership mode, entrepreneurs and their teams continually monitor motion in the operating environment within and outside the business, observing cues and clues that help anticipate their need to evolve.

Change leadership requires *organizational agility*, which means entrepreneurs and team members:

- Are attuned to continually evolving conditions within their business.
- Monitor subtle, gradual, rapid, or event-driven shifts in the external operating environment.
- Infer implications of environmental dynamics for their business.
- Adapt and adjust activities, resource allocation, and operating models as conditions change.
- Recognize change leadership is not an overlay to the business; it is the business.

McKinsey describes the agile organization as one which "demonstrates the ability to quickly reconfigure strategy, structure, processes, people, and technology toward value-creating and value-protecting opportunities."

Agile organizations are both stable and dynamic at the same time.

Consider large company examples like Amazon, Meta, Google, or JP Morgan Chase. In the words of hockey great Wayne Gretzky, they skate to where the puck (or the business) is going. Agility enables change leadership. It provides a foundation for leaders to build upon in developing the next chapter in an organization's story.

Developing your business's agility requires entrepreneurs to:
- Recognize the benefits of agility.
- Practice the observer view (if I were a neutral third-party observer, what would catch my attention as a possible change indicator?).
- Co-own identification of cues and clues prompting pre-emptive change with team members.

- Integrate gathering and interpreting environmental change indicators and identification of opportunities for pre-emptive change into business-as-usual activities.
- Own change leadership.

Where is your business today?

Here is a list of questions you and your team can use to foster conversation about your business's current level of agility, and inform next steps to raise organizational agility:

- How do we rate (high, medium, low) our company's level of agility today? In other words, how quickly do we reconfigure strategy, structure, processes, people and technology toward value-creating and value-protecting opportunities as conditions in our operating environment change?
- Which companies in our industry (or outside) demonstrate a high level of agility?
- What differences do we see between our company and the most agile companies?
- How does our company's current level of agility impact our customer experience?
- How does our company's current level of agility impact our employee experience?
- What risks are associated with our company's current level of agility?
- What would need to change at our company to rate your agility higher?

Effective change leadership requires creating and sustaining broad buy-in across stakeholders, inspiring participation in the transformation at hand, inviting co-ownership of tactics, and maintaining focus. Developing your company's organizational agility is a powerful step in elevating change leadership acumen.

Mind over (change) matter

At a recent Navigating Change® workshop, a regional manager shared that every time she introduces something new to her team, their first reaction is negative. It doesn't matter if the change was beneficial (say, a new technology or tool that makes it easier to perform certain tasks) or not; her team members tended to react negatively and resist the change. Most participants in the workshop echoed this pattern of reaction to change with their team members.

This type of negative response to change is not unusual. In fact, the well-researched condition known as Negativity Bias is a psychological phenomenon where humans give more weight to negative perceptions, experiences, information, or stimuli than to equally intense positive ones. Negativity Bias can contribute to strong emotional responses and impact judgment and decision-making, particularly in situations involving risk or uncertainty. The origins of this bias may be a variation of the fight-or-flight human wiring that helped prioritize threats to survival millions of years ago. What was beneficial in the era of wooly mammals contributes to organizational hurdles to navigating change today.

While Negativity Bias is prevalent, it is not the only point of resistance to change. *Change resistance* refers to the reluctance or opposition of individuals or teams within a firm to embrace and adapt to changes in processes, technologies, strategies, or organizational structure. Collective habits, routines, fears, and cultural characteristics can play into change resistance. Lack of trust in leadership, poor communications and lack of training and support make resistance to organizational change more challenging.

In the business world, the track record for successful change management is mixed at best. When it comes to navigating change, we know a great deal about what doesn't work:

- Failing to develop a clear picture of the business's future state.
- Failing to engage people across the business in co-owning a future-state vision.
- Failing to develop a deliberate road map between the current environment and future state.
- Failing to communicate frequently about progress and challenges in the journey.
- Failing to regularly re-engage the business and its' stakeholders in the future state vision.
- Failing to adjust the road map as conditions evolve.

Even with a well-documented body of knowledge about what doesn't work, there is a dearth of success stories when it comes to change management victories. Still, every organization is faced with navigating a continually changing operating environment.

Five fundamental factors are needed to overcome the inertia that stifles change programs — a clear future state vision, engagement, communication, actualization, and reinforcement. Every venture, be it a start-up or an ongoing enterprise, begins with a vision of what success looks like — what an organization wants to demonstrate. From there, engagement with key stakeholders — employees, partners, and owners — gives the change endeavor traction and sustainability. Frequent, regular communication with stakeholders about where the organization is going and about progress and accomplishments toward the vision creates transparency. Actualization brings specific results to life and highlights progress for the organization to observe. Reinforcement means frequent re-articulation of the vision, the road map to fulfill it and progress.

Here are specific steps leaders can take to help your team navigate change:

- **Recognize** the business world is in perpetual motion. Help your team reframe their view of change as an ongoing process, not an event. Recognizing that operating conditions are in perpetual motion helps align expectations and shift away from the false belief that the status quo means a static environment.
- **Unify** the team around your company's definition of what success looks like (aka your vision). The vision is like an organization's GPS – while conditions may change, the destination remains constant, and constancy empowers people in navigating change.
- **Declare** progress, milestones, successes, and setbacks. Declaration provides comfort through transparency. When these declarations are part of regular, ongoing communications, team members have an opportunity to embrace the message, even if it is related to a setback. There is a tendency for leaders to disregard setbacks, but that can contribute to distrust of leadership.
- **Repeat.** Repetition of these steps is essential in overriding the natural proclivity toward Negativity Bias and resistance to change. It's been said that more than 90% of our daily thoughts are repetitive, and 80% of repeated

thoughts are negative. If this view is even directionally correct, it means we need to invest heavily in highlighting the benefits of advancing our business in the direction of our vision. Until we develop mental and emotional engagement in the vision, navigating change among our team members is likely to remain stuck at the starting line.

Cues and Clues

Albert Einstein said, "The measure of intelligence is the ability to change." Change stimuli emerge in two manners – Systemic and Non-systemic cues. Systemic change cues impact all organizations – inflation, national or global economic expansion or contraction, tax code changes, pandemics, geopolitical issues, and the like. Non-systemic change cues are unique to a specific organization or industry. For instance: the patent on a company's flagship product expires next year allowing competitors to replicate that specific offering, or a new federal regulatory capital requirement which impacts all small, medium, and large banks.

An essential entrepreneurial practice is to identify relevant cues, then delve into underlying details to determine a level of urgency to address each condition:

Changing Demand

- What changes do you anticipate in your customer base over the next two to three years (demographics, geographic, economics)?
- What changes do you anticipate in customer expectations of your offering over the next two to three years (product, technology, ease of use, features, quality, pricing)?

- What have you tracked/observed with changes in customer satisfaction/engagement over the past two to three years?
- How has your customer attrition rate changed over the past two to three years?
- How has your flow of new customers changed over the past two to three years?
- What trends have you observed in the number of repeat customers over the past two to three years?
- What are the themes and volume associated with customer complaints over the past two to three years (including unfavorable online and social media traffic)?

Changing Supply

- What changes do you anticipate in employee expectations for your business over the next two to three years (evolution of the company's value proposition to employees, career and professional development, benefits, compensation)?
- How do you anticipate the talent pool (early, mid-career, seasoned talent) and competition for talent changing over the next two to three years?
- What have you tracked/observed with trend changes in employee engagement over the past two to three years?
- What was your level of employee attrition (regrettable, encouraging) over the past two to three years? How does this level align with your expectations?
- What themes and volume are associated with employee complaints over the past two to three years?

- What changes do you anticipate in suppliers over the next two to three years (supply chain changes, new suppliers, product offering, industry consolidation, technology, costs, pricing)?
- What types of non-systemic (e.g., unrelated to COVID-19 or inflation during the first half of the 2020s) supplier service/delivery issues have you experienced over the past two to three years? What is the cause?

Changing Customer Engagement Approaches

- What changes do you anticipate in how your company interfaces with customers (human interaction, physical sales/service locations, self-service, digital platforms)?
- What changes do you anticipate in the availability of on-demand customer engagement offerings (accessing your products or services where, when, and how the customer prefers)?
- What changes do you anticipate in the competitive landscape (new entrants, consolidation, new products, new technology, pricing changes) over the next two to three years, and how will these impact your business?
- What changes do you anticipate in how aggressively competitors pursue your customers over the next two to three years?
- What changes do you anticipate in your operating economics over the next two to three years?

Changing Technology

- What changes in technology do you anticipate will support your business operations (including sourcing, transportation, manufacturing, human resources, finance

and accounting, and marketing) over the next two to three years?
- What changes do you anticipate in the technology required to serve your customers?
- What changes do you anticipate in technology to engage with your suppliers and vendors?

Competition
- What changes do you anticipate in the competitive landscape (new entrants, consolidation, new products, new technology, pricing changes) over the next three years and how will these impact your business?
- What changes do you anticipate in how aggressively competitors pursue your clients over the next three years?
- What changes do you anticipate in your operating economics over the next three years?

This partial list of change cues suggests how entrepreneurs can evaluate the need and address evolving conditions with urgency. Knowing when to initiate change is essential in navigating change leadership.

Regardless of the change stimulus, in the business world entrepreneurs have an opportunity to anticipate and address their continually evolving environment for the benefit of their stakeholders. This means embracing the reality that business operating conditions are in perpetual motion. Those who do not heed the call to lead change as an ongoing process may jeopardize their organization's future.

Change leadership Tools

As a student of strategic management in graduate school, I learned four conversation starter questions for business leaders: Where are we now? (with our business), Where are we going? (aka: the vision), How will we get there? (the business operating model), and Where can we anticipate changes along the journey? The traditional SWOT analysis guides leaders in answering the first two questions but doesn't address questions three and four. The SWOT analysis captures existing strengths, weaknesses, opportunities, and threats, but falls short on incorporating future changes in customers, employees, technology, competition, and the overall operating environment.

The **Change Leadership Opportunity Assessment** (CLOA) was developed to guide leaders in evaluating leading and lagging indicators of the need to initiate business model changes. The CLOA's leading indicators are forward-looking signals suggesting future trends or outcomes. They aim to identify seeds of change before they become fully evident. Leading indicators are like the headlights on a car, illuminating the road ahead. Lagging indicators confirm trends that have already begun. Lagging indicators are like a car's rearview mirror, showing us where we've been.

Leading indicators suggesting the need to initiate business model changes include:
- Signals of changing customer mix or preferences
- Observed changes in customer or employee satisfaction or engagement
- Emerging technologies
- Changes in employee engagement
- New competitors

The Entrepreneur As Change Leader

- New products
- Increased complaints
- Unfavorable online and social media traffic
- Pricing deterioration

- The CLOA's lagging indicators include:
- Evidence of shifting demand
- Evidence of increasing supply of offerings like your company's
- Increases in customer attrition
- Increases in employee attrition
- Changes in the job applicant pool
- Increases in employee attrition
- Decline in repeat customers
- Increases in product returns
- Fewer new customers
- Decreasing average sales
- Margin deterioration

| Change Leadership Opportunity Assessment ||
Leading Indicators	Lagging Indicators (Reactive Change)
Indicators of changing customer preferences	Evidence of shifting demand
Observed changes in customer satisfaction or engagement	Evidence of increasing supply of offerings like your company's
Emerging technologies targeting all or part of your company's value proposition	Increasing regrettable employee attrition
Observed changes in employee engagement or satisfaction	Changes in size, qualifications of job applicant pool for open positions
Entry of new competitors to your market	Increasing customer attrition
Exit of existing competitors from your market	Decline in repeat customers
New products offered by competitors	Fewer new customers
Increased customer complaints	Decreasing average sales per customer
Unfavorable online and social media traffic	Margin deterioration
Pricing deterioration	Increasing product returns

The Entrepreneur's Journey

Each indicator is intended to focus an entrepreneur's attention on factors likely to necessitate a business model change. Early detection of changing conditions allows leaders time to explore strategic alternatives, which may not be available to the company over time.

The CLOA augments a traditional SWOT analysis by introducing dynamic elements of a business's operating environment. No single indicator (including the SWOT analysis) provides a complete picture. Using a combination of leading and lagging indicators, along with other data and analysis, prepares leaders to know when it's time for proactive change.

The Change Guidance Framework provides leaders with questions in seven areas of focus critical in navigating change. It begins with an inquiry into the future state picture and the organization's vision (what does success look like?). The Framework includes questions about co-ownership of the organization's vision, the roadmap from where the business is today, and its destination. Effective communications are core to every organization, so the Framework delves into the nature, content, and frequency of information flow. Navigating change always includes barriers to progress. The Framework encourages leaders to anticipate and prepare for inevitable barriers. As change leadership is an ongoing process, I include questions regarding sustainability. Finally, an organization's stakeholders need effective channels for feedback regarding how the business is showing up. Feedback Loop questions encourage leaders to actively seek and measure progress and perceptions from their constituents.

Focus	Questions

The Entrepreneur As Change Leader

Future State Picture	• What does success look like for this program? For the business overall? • How does the future state picture (vision) compare with the current environment? • What about the future state vision is compelling? Concerning? • How will our future state vision focus, guide daily activities?
Co-ownership	• What role will team members play in defining the future state picture? • How do we ensure broad co-ownership of our future state vision? • Which stakeholder group's buy-in is essential? Important? Beneficial? • What is our engagement governance approach?
Roadmap	• What are the specific areas of focus and activities to bridge the gap between the current environment and future state vision? • What are the workstreams necessary to address each area of focus? • How will we adjust the roadmap as conditions evolve?
Communication	• Who are our different audiences and how do communication needs differ for each group? • How will we approach initial program communication and messaging? • How will we approach ongoing program updates, progress and challenges throughout the journey? • What is the right frequency of communication?
Navigating Barriers	• What and where are anticipated barriers to advancing this program and how will we address them? • Where are known points of resistance to this program and how will we address them? • What is our governance approach to addressing unanticipated barriers and points of resistance?
Assuring Sustainability	• How will we ensure regular reengagement of the organization in fulfilling the future state vision? • How will we recognize and reward actions that advance the future state vision? • How will we address actions that do not align with advancing the future state vision? • How often will we meet as leaders to sustain engagement?
Feedback Loop	• What OKRs or deliverables will we measure and report on? • How will we elicit and assess stakeholder feedback throughout this program? • What mechanisms will we use to gather and share stakeholder feedback?

Why is Organizational Change a Challenge?

Change often involves disruption to the status quo. In its current usages, the term status quo means keeping things the same. However, the meaning has evolved over time. This Latin term translates to "the state in which things are." It was originally used in legal contexts to refer to the existing state of things that both parties agreed to maintain. Over time, the term broadened to describe the current situation in any context (not just legal or political). Noteworthy is that the original meaning did not imply steady state (not subject to change), rather simply the current state of conditions.

We are attracted to the stability of steady state conditions. Comfort anchored in conditions can only last if conditions are static. As conditions evolve (which is constant), a new normal is born. Still, "Status quo" is a Latin phrase that means "existing state of affairs."

In 1988, researchers William Samuelson and Richard Zeckhauser introduced the concept of Status Quo Bias - the preference for maintaining one's current situation and opposing actions that may change that situation. Status quo bias is a cognitive bias based on emotion.

Samuelson and Zeckhauser's academic article "Status Quo Bias in Decision-Making"[23] discussed a series of decision-making experiments. This research found that when given a choice between the status quo and a new option, individuals were more likely to stick with what they already knew. This bias negatively affects our ability to make decisions. Our desire for a steady state

---

[23] https://www.researchgate.net/publication/5152072_Status_Quo_Bias_in_Decision-Making

may prevent us from evaluating emerging options objectively, leading to missed opportunities and elevated risk due to inaction. Status quo bias can have a deleterious impact on a business when it prevents adaptation as operating conditions evolve.

Comfort in current conditions blends with fear of the unknown, comfort with the status quo, lack of understanding of the reasons behind impending changes, lack of clarity about what success looks like, or individual behavioral styles. Our brains are wired to seek familiarity and stability. When conditions contradict these anchors, we can feel anxious and apprehensive. It's easy to be emotionally attached to our routines, even when they no longer align with our individual needs.

Then, there is the behavioral science around loss aversion. Humans tend to prioritize avoiding losses over the potential for receiving gains (like the risk aversion dimension of status quo bias). Perceptions about potential losses associated with change - disrupted routines, loss of control, or failure – may outweigh the perceived benefits.

These factors, and individual behavioral styles, like a natural proclivity toward predictability and consistency, can contribute to habitual resistance. Changing habits requires a clear replacement habit, motivation, incentive, and continuous reinforcement.

When we move from individual factors affecting navigating change to those at the organizational level, it's like moving from basic math to multivariate calculus. An organization is simply a community of individuals. What is true at the individual level about change is exponentially amplified at the organizational level.

Change resistance refers to reluctance or opposition of individuals or teams within a firm to embrace and adapt to changes in processes, technologies, strategies, or organizational structure. Collective habits, routines, fears, and cultural characteristics can play into change resistance. At the leadership level of a company, lack of trust in leadership, poor communications, and lack of training and support make resistance to organizational change more challenging.

I worked with an independent bank that recently changed CEOs. They created multiple vision statements, but they weren't what employees could articulate or aspire to. The bank had no clear value proposition (little consistency across the institution about why customers would choose this bank, or their differentiation). Perhaps to no surprise, the business model was fragmented; it was unclear if the bank's focus was business-to-consumer (B2C), business-to-business (B2B), or business-to-business-to-consumer (B2B2C).

After 45 days of deep-dive sessions with leaders, team members, partners, customers, former employees, and board members, we advanced a set of foundational agreements. First, the bank operated as a B2B2C service provider; it only interacted with end-user customers through other businesses. Rather than seeing these other businesses as "internal clients," the bank redefined these relationships as partnerships. Second, given the B2B2C business model, the bank refined their vision, recognizing that their definition of success needed to include value for their partners as well as the end-user customers. Third, a set of five priorities was established and distilled into a strategic roadmap for the bank.

The Entrepreneur As Change Leader

Sidenote: Addressing the vision *after* addressing the business operating model may sound inconsistent with the *vision first* recommendation in previous chapters. In this specific case, the level of confusion experienced following the previous CEO's departure required triage, beginning with clearly answering the question: What business are we in? That line of inquiry led to addressing the business model first, then refining existing vision statements into a single, engaging definition of success for the bank.

The bank's new strategic plan and associated funding was unanimously approved by their board for immediate implementation. The leadership team was pleased with their work, and ready to begin implementation. Then, seemingly out of nowhere, the Groundhog Day scenario began.

Members of the bank's leadership team who were actively engaged in vision development, business model definition and strategic plan detailing suddenly began resisting implementation. In some cases, resistance was direct and blatant – "nobody really believes in this plan," "we've tried all this before, and it won't work," "the board of directors doesn't have a clue about what really happens in our business," or "all of the best people in the bank will leave and go to a better firm as soon as they have a chance." In other cases, resistance was much more nuanced – "our old CEO was on the right track, she just needed more time to move things forward," "things aren't as bad as the board makes it sound; they just need more data," and "I think we need to take the next few months to analyze our business in more depth before we make any changes,"

These reactions and resistance seemed inconsistent with the energy applied to the plan development process. Through in-depth analysis, we learned the stakeholders demonstrating greatest resistance to change were members of the bank's leadership team (the very people that co-created the bank's new roadmap).

To help uncover individual challenges to advancing the bank's new strategic plan, we engaged a DISC Certified Trainer. DISC is a behavioral self-assessment tool developed by psychologist William Moulton Marston, based on his emotional and behavioral theory published in 1928. The DISC assessment is designed to anticipate job performance by categorizing individuals' natural behavioral styles into four characteristics – Dominance (direct, strong-willed, forceful, fast-paced, skeptical), Influence (sociable, talkative, lively, fast-paced and accepting), Steadiness (gentle, accommodating, soft-hearted, cautious, and accepting) and Conscientious (private, analytical, logical, cautious, and skeptical).

DISC profiles for the bank's 22 managers led to an aha moment. Global DISC distribution data indicates 9% of the population has Dominance as their primary style; 29% Influence; 32% Steadiness; and 30% Conscientious. However, at this bank, 90% – 20 of these 22 managers – had a single behavioral style – Conscientious as their top style, followed by Steadiness as the second. This is statistically highly unusual, and important in understanding these leaders' resistance to change.

According to the DISC style descriptions, people with a Conscientious/Steadiness behavioral style highly value stability, minimizing risk, and experiencing reliable, consistent outcomes. They tend to be cautious, reflective, stable, reliable, orderly, careful, and conventional.

The Entrepreneur As Change Leader

Remarkable! Ninety percent of the bank's leaders had individual behavioral styles resistant to change. In aggregate, this amplified common challenges associated with navigating change. The solution for this bank was to create a series of steps to develop agility acumen among its leaders. The program, anchored in the company's vision and values, supported advancement of the new business model.

The takeaway from this case study for change leaders is this: While there are many factors which contribute to the challenge of change - comfort in current conditions, fear of the unknown, lack of understanding of the reasons supporting changes – the human element, and individual behavioral styles in particular, must be recognized and fully addressed for successful change leadership.

What can Entrepreneurs do to Elevate their Success with Change Leadership?

Recognize it for what it is – Changing conditions can include process redesign, new technology and tools, or a refined go-to-market model. Whatever is included, there is always a behavioral change element to change management. According to Professor Megan Call[24] at the University of Utah, "Behavior change is complicated and complex because it requires a person to disrupt a current habit while simultaneously fostering a new, possibly unfamiliar, set of actions. This process takes time, usually longer than we prefer."

When entrepreneurs recognize part of their role (as change leaders) is to invite, support and facilitate behavioral change, it

---

[24] https://accelerate.uofuhealth.utah.edu/resilience/why-is-behavior-change-so-hard#:~:text=Behavior change is complicated and usually longer than we prefer.

can clarify what's necessary to advance the business and traverse forces that reinforce the status quo.

Act accordingly – When entrepreneurs understand the core elements required to stimulate behavioral change, they can align their energy with actions to support team members. Taking steps to (1) align the change effort with a clear description of success, (2) create co-ownership in the change initiative, (3) initiate relevant tasks, behavioral and social communications, (4) earn and sustain engagement in bringing the future-state vision to life will enhance the organization's change acumen.

Identify opportunities for self-initiated disruption– Disruption happens. It's a natural force as industries evolve. John F. Kennedy said, "Change is the law of life. And those who look only to the past or present are certain to miss the future."

Capitalizing on perpetual motion, innovators create industry disruption to address evolving customer needs, interests, and preferences. At the same time, many businesses let change take them by surprise. Knowing the dynamic nature of business, and the continuous redefinition of "normal," entrepreneurs have a decision to make—initiate change and innovate or react to external pressures. Self-initiated disruption serves two purposes. First, it preempts external disruption by existing competitors and new entrants to your business. Second, it grounds the organization in its reason for existing through the employees, customers, and stakeholders served.

Integrate preemptive change opportunity identification into regular business operating reviews – Broaden standard quarterly financial performance reviews to include conversations about indicators of changing customer needs, preferences, trends, operational improvement opportunities, new

The Entrepreneur As Change Leader

technologies applicable to your business, new vendor practices, and the like. This will identify seeds with the potential to grow into full-blown paradigm shifts for your organization.

Recognize change leadership is part of *leadership* and own it – French philosopher Rene Descartes wrote that if you choose not to decide, you still have made a choice. All leaders need to adjust to a rapidly changing environment, and choosing not to act is rarely a good option. In the context of perpetual change, develop your organization's acumen in *leading change*. Champion a vision of where the organization is going in the evolution of who you serve and how you deliver to your customers and build esprit de corps with agility as a core competency.

Chapter 9
Closing thoughts: The Entrepreneur's Operating System

Making Your Business Work for You

Entrepreneurship is not a single breakthrough moment. It is a disciplined rhythm. Throughout this book, we have explored the fundamentals that make a business sustainable, scalable, and resilient in a business world defined by perpetual motion:

- Know your customer
- Define success clearly
- Build and refine your plan
- Design and manage your go-to-market model
- Lead with alignment and discipline
- Work on your business as well as in your business
- Own change leadership

Now it is time to distill everything into a practical, repeatable operating system. This chapter is your field manual.

One Connecting Principle Behind Everything

Remember this central truth: Entrepreneurs do not work for themselves. They work for their customers. Revenue is evidence of relevance to your customers. If relevance erodes, diminishing results typically follow.

Most entrepreneurs navigate three seasons in their business's life:

1. **Early Stage** – Proving viability
2. **Scaling** – Building systems and discipline
3. **Stuck** – Plateaued, misaligned, or drifting

Throughout these seasons, fundamentals do not change, but emphasis does.

PART I: If You're Early Stage

Your focus: **Earn relevance before you scale complexity.**

1. Clarify the Problem Before Perfecting the Product

Ask:
- What problem are we solving?
- Who urgently wants this solved?
- What are they currently doing instead?
- Why would they switch to our solution?
- Will they pay for our solution?

If you cannot answer these clearly, stop building and start validating.

Action:
- Conduct 25–50 real customer conversations.
- Test market before you scale.
- Refine your offering based on feedback, not your passion for the product or service.

2. Define Your Serviceable Obtainable Market (SOM)

Don't chase TAM wishful thinking numbers.

Focus on:
- Who can you realistically reach at this point in time?
- With what budget?
- Through which channels?
- In what time frame?

Action:
- Define your Target Customer Profile in one page.
- Identify the top three channels to reach them.

Closing Thoughts: The Entrepreneur's Operating System

- Track conversion rates (prospect to bon fide customer) from day one.

3. Choose How You Compete

You cannot be a Low-cost leader, Premium differentiator, Product innovator, or Niche specialist all at once. Pick your lane and stay with it until or unless your growth trajectory suggests it's time for a change.

Action:
- Write a one-sentence competitive positioning statement: "We serve ___ by delivering ___ better than ___."

If your sentence is unclear, it's likely your strategy is unclear.

4. Build a Simple Plan — Review Every 90 Days

Early-stage planning should be clear and disciplined.

Include:
- Revenue target
- Customer acquisition goal
- Key assumptions
- Top 3 priorities
- Quarterly Key Performance Indicators

Action:
- Implement a 90-day review cadence.
- Ask: What did we learn? What must change?

Early-Stage Warning Signs

You are drifting if:
- You are building more than you are selling.
- You are chasing investor praise instead of customer revenue.
- You describe features more than outcomes.
- Your priorities change weekly.

The Entrepreneur's Journey

PART II: If You're Scaling

Your focus: Replace improvisation with intentional design.

Growth exposes weaknesses and gaps in your operating model.

1. Document Your Go-to-Market Model

Your business model must now be explicit.
Clarify:
- Target customers
- Customer experience and engagement approach
- Value proposition
- Core processes
- Economic model
- Talent expectations
- All these elements matter when you start your business. They require review, revalidation, and refinement if necessary, as you scale. If the answer to the question – what is your customer experience? - is "It depends," you have a model problem.
- Action:
- Document your end-to-end customer journey.
- Identify points of inconsistency.
- Standardize the experience.

2. Develop a Playbook

Scaling without a playbook leads to chaos.
Define:
- Roles and responsibilities
- Performance metrics
- Customer engagement standards
- Process workflows

Closing Thoughts: The Entrepreneur's Operating System

Action:
- Build a simple internal operating manual.
- Train to it.
- Manage to it.
- Coach to it.

3. Audit Alignment with Vision

As companies scale, scope creep often happens.
Ask:
- What are we doing that does not align with our vision?
- Which customers are least profitable?
- Which activities are resource drains?

Action:
- Rank current initiatives High/Medium/Low alignment with your vision.
- Eliminate or delegate Low alignment activities.

4. Strengthen the Right Bottom Line

Financial reviews are not strategic reviews. Go deeper:
- Why are customers buying?
- Which segments are most profitable?
- What behavior drives our profitable growth?
- Where are we cross-subsidizing losses?

Action:
- Leverage the Pareto concept by identifying the top 20% of customers generating 80% of profits.
- Design strategy around them.
- Evaluate the best approach to dealing with unprofitable customers and execute.

Scaling Warning Signs

You are drifting if:

- You spend more time firefighting than executing your operating plan.
- Customer experience varies widely.
- Hiring is reactive, not strategic.
- Revenue grows but profitability stagnates.

PART III: If You're Stuck

Your focus: Reclaim relevance.

Plateaus are rarely caused by effort, rather misalignment.

1. Revisit the Vision

Ask:
- Does our definition of success (vision) still fit?
- Are we behaving like the company we say we want to be?

If vision is unclear, everything fragments.

Action:
- Rewrite your vision in one sentence.
- Ensure it is aspirational, inspirational, and actionable.

2. Diagnose Root Cause — Not Symptoms

Revenue decline is not the root cause. Customer attrition is not the root cause. Margin pressure is not the root cause.

Ask:
- What changed in customer expectations?
- What changed in competition?
- What changed in our delivery?

Action:
- Interview lost customers.

Closing Thoughts: The Entrepreneur's Operating System

- Interview your best customers.
- Identify gaps between the two groups.

3. Practice Self-Initiated Disruption

Do not wait to be disrupted.
Ask:
- If we started today, would we design this same business model?
- Which "sacred cows" in our business need questioning?
- What would we eliminate?
- What new areas of value for our customers will we explore?

Action:
- Conduct a business model redesign exercise.
- Imagine a competitor building a model to replace you by capitalizing on your company's shortcomings as conditions have shifted, then bridge the gaps between your offering today and what customers expect.

4. Remove Activities That Don't Play to Strength

Struggle often signals misalignment.
Ask:
- What do we do exceptionally well?
- What should someone else do better?

Action:
- Outsource, automate, or eliminate non-core activities.
- Double down on core strengths.

Stuck Warning Signs

- Growth has plateaued for 18+ months.
- You keep solving the same problems repeatedly.

- Your best people feel disengaged.
- Customers negotiate on price more than before.
- You see evidence of your offering slipping behand customer expectations.

The Entrepreneur's Weekly Discipline

Regardless of season, implement this rhythm:
Weekly:
- Review KPIs tied to relevance.
- Ask: What did we learn about our customer this week?

Monthly:
- Review customer wins and losses.
- Audit strategic priority alignment.

Quarterly:
- Reassess top 3 strategic priorities.
- Review competitive positioning.

Annually:
- Reaffirm vision.
- Revisit business model.
- Redesign where needed.
- Planning is not a document. It is an ongoing, dynamic process entrepreneurs must own.

The Entrepreneurial Leadership Imperative

Entrepreneurial leadership is not about control. It is about clarity.
Clarity of:
- Customer
- Vision
- Priorities
- Model
- Expectations
- Change

Closing Thoughts: The Entrepreneur's Operating System

You are the navigator. Conditions will change. Winds will shift. Competitors will appear and disappear. Technology will evolve. Your role is not to eliminate uncertainty. It is to lead through it.

The Test

Your business is working for you when:
- Revenue is predictable.
- Customers return and refer.
- Margins support reinvestment.
- You spend more time designing the future than fixing the past.
- Your team understands the vision.
- Decisions align naturally.
- You are not trapped in daily chaos.

If this is not yet your reality, the fundamentals in this book are your blueprint.

Closing Reflection Questions

As you process ideas that resonate with you from this book, take time to answer these exploration questions:
- Who specifically is our target customer?
- What is the need or issues our target customer wants to address?
- What do they value?
- What will our customer pay for the value we deliver?
- How do we differentiate our offering clearly?
- Is our business model intentionally designed?
- Are we reviewing and refining our business model consistently?
- What activities should we stop?

- What strengths should we amplify?
- What will our business look like three years from now if we stay on our current path?
- What must change beginning today?

The Entrepreneur's Commitment

The entrepreneur's journey is a noble one. Founders, innovators, businesspeople are in search of making a meaningful impact and earning a reward invest passion, time, and energy to bring their ideas to life. Success in this journey is not an event. It is a process of preparation, discipline, and fundamentals practiced daily. The journey favors those who master the basics, refine continuously, lead intentionally, serve relentlessly, and adapt proactively.

These actions, performed consistently, are the necessary steps to make your business work for you. This is the Entrepreneur's Journey. And it begins anew today.

www.ingramcontent.com/pod-product-compliance
Lightning Source LLC
Chambersburg PA
CBHW071543220526
45469CB00003B/905